MOTHER WINTER

a memoir

SOPHIA SHALMIYEV

Simon & Schuster
New York   London   Toronto   Sydney   New Delhi

Simon & Schuster
1230 Avenue of the Americas
New York, NY 10020

First Simon & Schuster hardcover edition February 2019

SIMON & SCHUSTER and colophon are registered trademarks of Simon & Schuster, Inc.

For information about special discounts for bulk purchases, please contact Simon & Schuster Special Sales at 1-866-506-1949 or business@simonandschuster.com.

The Simon & Schuster Speakers Bureau can bring authors to your live event. For more information or to book an event, contact the Simon & Schuster Speakers Bureau at 1-866-248-3049 or visit our website at www.simonspeakers.com.

Interior design by Carly Loman

Manufactured in the United States of America

10 9 8 7 6 5 4 3 2 1

Library of Congress Cataloging-in-Publication Data

Names: Pfaff-Shalmiyev, Sophia, 1978- author.
Title: Mother winter : a memoir / Sophia Shalmiyev.
Description: First Simon & Schuster hardcover edition. | New York : Simon & Schuster, 2019.
Identifiers: LCCN 2018016724| ISBN 9781501193088 (hardcover) | ISBN 9781501193095 (trade paper) | ISBN 9781501193101 (ebook)
Subjects: LCSH: Pfaff-Shalmiyev, Sophia, 1978- | Pfaff-Shalmiyev, Sophia, 1978—Family. | Russians—Oregon—Biography. | Immigrants—Oregon—Biography. | Mothers and daughters—Russia (Federation)—Biography. | Return migration—Russia (Federation)—Biography.
Classification: LCC F885.R9 P43 2019 | DDC 305.9/06912—dc23
LC record available at https://lccn.loc.gov/2018016724

ISBN 978-1-5011-9308-8
ISBN 978-1-5011-9310-1 (ebook)

This book is dedicated to all the feminist
mothers and the girls who need them most.
And to my dearest Jake and Frances.

When a woman drinks it's as if an animal were drinking, or a child. Alcoholism is scandalous in a woman, and a female alcoholic is rare, a serious matter. It's a slur on the divine in our nature.

—MARGUERITE DURAS

I

Russian sentences begin backward.

When I learned English well enough to love it, I realized my inner tongue was running in the wrong direction. As does the Old Testament, the one *we* don't call the good book. The one that became the bad, forbidden book, and is read back to front. The period blood came right after I began practicing my American accent in eighth grade: all smudged red clots to brown waste.

I have been teaching my daughter to wipe herself front to back to avoid the chronic infections her body is prone to. She squats and glares at me, then follows her instinct for revolt no matter the aftermath.

The daughters who live in flashbacks will suspend their tongues between the origin and the destination—the past more immediate, more urgent than any new day. "Mother, loosen my tongue or adorn me with a lighter burden." Even Audre Lorde needs her mother's permission to grease the gears on the train to the beginning, to knock on coffins.

I worship the flaneurs and flaneuses, those who stroll about the city—especially the women who dare to walk alone at night and then write about it. But those who slink around with too little purpose or not enough clothing to cover their bodies are marked as streetwalkers, or *shlyuchas*. This was one of your labels in my home. There may be no records, beyond arrests or death certificates, of a *shlyucha*'s gallivanting.

I don't worship my real mother, but I can't get her buttermilk smell off my mouth.

Almost all of the paper that contains your name was flushed down the toilet, lost, thrown away, or hidden like a lover who buries her face in the pillow when coming. All the letters I secretly wrote you were in English, and if I knew where to send them you would have needed an auxiliary, a translator to convert my scribbles into our mother tongue. I didn't bother practicing my Russian on you. That river was dammed with teenage hormones and hopes of fitting in, a changeling in America. There was no address in Russia to mail anything to, and then I knew only your maiden name, Danilova, as well as the married-and-divorced-from name we shared at one time, Shalmiyeva.

I heard rumors that you had remarried and divorced twice since my father took you to court and the judge ruled you an unfit mother in the early 1980s. My uncle visited you in 1995 before he joined us on a visa in Brooklyn, but I only found out about these cordial gatherings a few years ago. At the time you sat in your St. Petersburg apartment looking frail and famished, close to our old place on Bronnitskaya, in what used to be Leningrad, I was a junior deciding between Reed and Evergreen colleges, editing a high school feminist newspaper, listening to riot grrrl bands, writing poems for you, and auditioning surrogate mothers for myself: feminists, writers, activists, painters, ballbusters, killjoys, sex workers, gay men.

And so, I assembled a fantasy caretaker army of mostly loose and tragic women mixed with audacious and assertive ones—a hologram of what I imagined you would be like if I hadn't been *stolen* from you. If you hadn't left me for the bottle long before my father took me away to America eleven-years-your-daughter.

Elena. Mother. Mama. You.

I choose You.

II

In photos, Elena looks like Marguerite Duras on the cover of her book *The Lover*, which begins appropriately enough with a man pleased that the beautiful girl's face has been "ravaged" and torn apart by time and alcohol. The heroine disappears and becomes an old woman after he stops gorging on her young body. His age will forever remain irrelevant.

You are blessed with an ageless ambiguity. Every child looks up at their mother and thinks whatever age this woman might be, it is surely the right number, the most radiant phase of her life as their mirror. The perpetual contact, the mutual gazing, give no pause big enough for a child to contemplate the mother as separate from herself for some time to come.

Mother is a circle—a complete and perfect hole.

× × × ×

Elena has vanished, and I need her back.

The last time we saw each other you were thirty years old, all eyes and mouth, both painted dark and begging to be let in the house. You came in and robbed my dad's girlfriend, Luda. You said that you were going to a rehab in Sochi; the mineral baths would help you with the morning shakes.

You needed a bathing suit and some clothes. You were envious of the hairspray your junior substitute managed to procure on the black market. You took the bow-shaped, silver-colored, plastic hairpin Luda had given me for my birthday and it sat on the front of your head like a half-hung hammock, not quite attached, as you went through the shelves. You opened your mouth and spritzed the hair lacquer down your throat and swallowed hard; a pinkish hue returned to your winter-dull cheeks.

You filled up two bags with Luda's belongings and kissed me goodbye. I told you to hurry up and leave before they got back. I was afraid of what would happen to you more than I was of the punishment I realized was now imminent for me. My father refused to let me see you ever again after that day. He couldn't risk getting his passport stolen as our plans to fly overseas solidified.

Question, question, thump, thump, why don't you answer me, my father pleads as he grabs me by the collar and brings me to his face, shakes me with feet dangling in the air, shoulder blades scraping the wallpaper, before he throws me onto his bed in frustration. I'm telling the truth of a broken compass. Below the quiet, below the silence, under the dust of muteness—a shell, shocked.

When the ambulance comes we tell them I was climbing where I shouldn't have been. The tall white willow-tree bodies of adults bending over me wonder if I can walk. I can crawl on all fours to go to the toilet after a few days. I am upright within two weeks, using a walker and then just lying on my stomach while my dad intermittently brings a whole fish out of the freezer and it burns the heat of the hurt worse than the bruise did alone.

Humans should never touch a baby bird that fell from her nest. Like when I fake-fell from the wardrobe chest, sustaining an L4 fracture in my back, the place where I was cracked against the wooden edge of my father's bed because I lied and said I didn't let my mother in the house; I didn't let her make off with those bags of clothes.

x x x x

A mother who won't return has holy water she drinks in the morning to cure hangovers; her own mother and grandmother to live and drink with when her husband is forced to get legal help and kick her out for not coming home at night; a daughter to wake up in the middle of the night to rob the Lenin memorial in the town square of all of its tulips; mornings with bedbug welts and a room filled with heaps of stolen flowers on each shelf, table, and windowsill; a white rabbit fur coat with a sleeve that hangs on by a pin; pouty lips painted with dark-brown lipstick; men's cologne to force down when out of vodka; thin blue veins on stark white breasts; horny soldiers who wink and whistle at her in the street.

Loitering. Roaming. Lurking. Stalking.

III

Elena drank in the midst of a modified version of a prohibition. The dry laws of 1985 meant alcohol was to be sold in limited quantities during shortened hours of operation. Visible intoxication was grounds for arrest. The USSR under Gorbachev's Perestroika was a country consumed with tackling its public health crisis and restoring the welfare and dignity that were hardly ever there to begin with. Russians were used to a system of rations already, so it wasn't shocking to an average citizen that there would be a cap on how much booze they could purchase a month, unless they had a genuine dependence, which was sort of the point of this initiative. Gorbachev was a visionary, a man ahead of his time who dared to introduce ideas of cooperative commerce, freedom of speech, and functional socialism to a weary and calloused population conditioned to expect gulags as the antidote to dissent. The leader whose talents and grace we squandered shortly before the country crumbled, as Reagan licked his lips and smacked his knee, understood that domestic violence and most street crime were the result of chronic alcoholism, but the lashes of war and poverty reimagined as valiance were too raw for Soviets to blister over.

My mother's family lived through the Leningrad Blockade of the Great Patriotic War and drank to celebrate having survived the bombardments and lack of bread as much as to forget them. They smoked harsh and dirt-cheap unfiltered cigarettes called *papirosyuh*. They knew how to make their own brew and didn't need much to get by, so the system of rations didn't affect them as much as it did others. The elder women wore itchy gray shawls cross-wrapped in the front and tied in the back seemingly year-round and slept with boots, *valenkis*, on every night—restrained, alert, ready for anything, and apparently always cold. They kept their faith and tolerated Jews, whom they blamed for the war. To the Russians who were getting shelled because the Germans were hunting down *an inferior blood*, their Christian sons and husbands lost on the battlefields, their daughters dragging around frozen siblings on sleds that used to make them scream with glee going down the hill, it felt like yet another sacrifice, unworthy collateral damage, an unfair trade.

Russian Christians cross themselves the opposite way, like Jews reading right to left, so they have their backwardness in common.

A song, almost like a nursery rhyme, I heard in my youth was about Jews having the calloused claw of an ostrich from counting and hiding money all day. My great-granny sang the lyrics and laughed, patting me on the head with a benign sincerity, as if to say, "Don't take it to heart, my tiny black ostrich."

× × × ×

There were two things my father and I didn't talk about in the old Communist country—my alcoholic mother, and God. The itinerant presence and enforced absence of each were so vividly incongruent and interchangeable as to appear banal. One seemed no more probable than the other.

She was a pantry-moth mother. Stuck mottled in sacks of grain. Everyone, encumbered, tattle-telling the truth about her. Trying to clean her out of their dark closets. A nuisance. Spat out a daughter so intractable she keeps walking into her father's hand until it slaps her chin to chest. Passed on a fascial hostility in lieu of a hope chest or a dowry. An ice snap in their connective tissue. Bones cracking like winter branches. Mean to the marrow.

Dad never got wintery feet about keeping his little girl when his wife ran back to her mother's house. He turned in stacks of documents from Elena's hospital stays where she had her delirium tremens as evidence of her inability to go on with the duties of a parent. With the help of a determined public defender who agreed with my dad's sentiment that "Woman Chronic Alcoholism, Stage II, is more severe and tragic than in a man," he claimed me for his own, unheard of in Russia for a young man. The fog of war of their custody battles meant we didn't retreat from the story of her as the clear enemy.

My granny Galina wanted to adopt me, or at least to fight for partial custody on her maligned daughter's behalf. Instead of taking me to court when I was in first grade, she and my dad sat on opposite sides of our living room and asked me to walk to the one I would choose to live with if I could. I stayed put at the center of the room with my head down. My dad asked me if I wanted to go live with my granny. Do I choose them over him? My father was as dependable as the dawn. My mother was a mythical beached mermaid swimming home from the bar in the dark. I didn't dare speak—a turncoat in a hair shirt. "Silence equals consent," Dad groaned, arms folded, shaking his head in protest of this perceived treason.

But dead foremothers speak. "There ain't no answer. There ain't gonna be any answer. There never has been an answer. That's the answer," Gertrude Stein will whisper in my sore ear many years later.

When Elena wouldn't show up for work at the telephone company it was suggested *she quit cavorting and either get sober or face termination.* A doublethink mother, she entered the pit of withdrawals to buy herself time in the real world, to simulate a fresh start, to come over to her former apartment and play long-lost mother to a daughter who was frightened of her return. So afraid the earth under her feet would quake by her mother's reemergence, she would have rather slid around low to the ground and hid in the goo of wet reeds like a river snake.

× × × ×

Soviets discussed theology as a marketing tool for the naive and greedy masses who prayed for themselves only, gave up their lives to a ghost, and lived by a set of rules in a book that hindered scientific inquiry. God as foe. The rational Communists declaring checkmate.

Most churches were blown up or repurposed after the Russian Revolution. The grand ones endured as national showcases of our architectural prowess. Minor ones weren't worth the all-seeing eyes of the Red Army.

The Second World War took more of these houses of worship in air raids, but some became war rooms or holding pens for prisoners. The Germans maintained their efficiency quotas and pushed whole villages of people inside churches, locked them in, and lit the stacks of hay outside with their torches.

My matrilineal, pious stock continued to sneak into the extant churches, ignored or secretly revered as unofficial keepers of an underground system. They were the Old Believers.

× × × ×

Superstitions remain vital to Russians, especially to the nouveau riche, who are going back to Orthodoxy in droves with a nostalgic yearning to rewrite the Russian Revolution and give the spoils of victory to the White Army. It is difficult to believe that post-Soviet

Russians can exist in the present any easier than those who fought in the Second World War. Yesterday has never ended.

Epigenetics postulates that people who live in constant fear for generations believe they will never cease being persecuted. With a viscous terror ever-present in their bodies, it would seem like they have earned the right to escape, it's their reward for becoming an involuntary hiccup inside of a putrid memory.

"One of the hallmarks of trauma is the loss of the ability to plan for the future. It's really about the loss of control," says Masha Gessen of Russians who must tough it out under a new dictator, to feign amnesia. The Soviet Union ultimately sold itself out for shopping malls with plentiful blue jeans with ghastly embellishments to offset their previous austere uniforms.

My father was a benevolent dictator, but the tyranny trickled down from her house key turning our lock the wrong way on random mornings instead of lighting a match to the stove to warm up some kasha for the family.

Dad went by four names throughout his life: Gavriil, his birth name. Grisha, his nickname. Gregory, his formal name. And eventually, Gabriel—his Americanized, polished, and most palatable self. Gabriel means "God is my strength" in Hebrew. My father, the archangel protector in the Bible charged with being a messenger, wanted me to marry a nice Jewish boy, a Russian he could talk with freely using shorthand and common jokes; a survivor's view of the world.

But I fell in love with an American whose family is Lutheran of German descent.

Gabriel planted himself outside a locked bedroom door of his house the day I told him I would be getting married. The door shook from his sobs as he spoke to someone, to me, to God, to himself. This was a betrayal he had committed twice, going outside of his faith, his community, and his tribe. He promised to disown me if I went through with the proposal. I could still correct his mistakes and continue our lineage the proper way, with a Jewish man, doggedly ambitious, established and driven, truly worthy of our family and me. He begged this way until my stepmother came to my rescue and dragged him away, whispering that his protests would only serve to push me further away. Dad and Luda will end up walking me down a grass aisle to a rain-soaked chuppah, all rows put aside.

Mike and I will have two children—a boy, Jake, a girl, Frances—both baptized, even though we have no real faith of our own. We spawned what my great-granny may have called little gray ostrich babies, a new breed of in-betweenness, of absorbing enemy lines.

Gabriel remains at his post, even when locked out.

IV

Your ex-husband was a hypnotic father, an actual hypnotist by the time he finished school and became a psychotherapist. He took me to work at his clinic sometimes and I sat in on his séances, where he rocked back and forth putting a spell on men with numb left arms, chest pains, phobias, disorders of the nervous system.

I snuck out and walked the halls lined with glass-case displays of glistening bread and wreaths of wheat, symbols of our storied Russian labor force. I would peek into all of the different treatment rooms. Paraffin dips. Iodine rubs. Mineral water cures. Acupuncture needles attached to electric wires.

If she wasn't busy I would say hello to the speech therapist I often visited for my impediment, mispronouncing the letter *L*. The chalkboard in our sessions was dominated by the Cyrillic *L*, shaped like a house. So essential to enunciating your name, Elena. Or the word for love, *lyublyu*.

The Russian *L* looks like an American *A*, without a belt.

The Russian *L* is an empty American *A*. Without containment. No mother. No home. The Daughter can't utter her name without swallowing the letter like tepid pureed soup. The speech therapist asking, "Please touch your teeth. Do you hear yourself? You make it sound like a *V*."

But the phantom mother and the tongue-tied daughter share a mute *V*. An upside-down Russian *L*. The shape of their sex. The American cunt of her future. Victory. Freedom without freedom.

× × × ×

It was too risky to ask for her and be denied so I didn't say her name much. *Mother, loosen my tongue.*

I was scared of us being seen together, scared to sit next to her and be aligned with an outcast. Most of all, I didn't want to betray my father's girlfriend, who judged Elena without pity. A generous scarcity of mercy. My mother must have felt humiliated. She must have given up on herself completely. She must have retreated and relapsed even harder. How small she looked sitting on that couch, reaching out for my hand.

When my mother was allowed a visit, I swatted her away as she shrank into her seat. I stared toward the door, tortured her with prolonged silence. I worried that if I sat on her lap, if I hugged her, if I sided with her in front of my dad and future stepmom, I would fall through a dank well in her chest and she would leave again. I would be banished to live in her chest like a traitor, an outsider, nomadic roadkill.

A returned check. Null and void. A zero would be my number. I would be vanished.

V

Girl is a four-letter word.

Four is the only number in the English language that is self-contained and holds the clue to its function, being made up of four letters. No other number does this.

Russians are scrupulous followers of numerology, tea-leaf readings, evil-eye spells. We believe that good luck can be lost if you're not paying attention to a coded system, one passed down to you generationally.

You can also fail to collect on your good fortune if you do not remain vigilant and know what to look for. Most of the superstitions are about launching your journey.

Before you set off for the airport you must sit on your suitcases. This way you are able to think and leave your troubles behind.

If you forget something inside when you're already out the door you must go look at yourself in the mirror upon reentry. This way you make it back home in one piece.

It is best to have a family member, or a friend, splash a jug of water on the back of your car as you drive off. This purifies your voyage, providing you with a clean slate.

× × × ×

We once left Russia; I once came back. When I returned to Russia in 2004, determined to find you and bring you back home with me like a lost puppy stuffed in a sack, everyone in my family refused to sit on suitcases for good luck. There was unanimous disappointment at my decision to waste time and money on a lost cause. There were murmurs of ethnic cleansing, hate crimes, and kidnappings.

Russian Orthodoxy Believers call death a homecoming.

My father's friends took turns telling their own stories of rough muggings, assaults that ran the gamut from being choked in an alley for a gold watch to pistol whipped in a stairwell for an engagement ring in a corrupt and unruly country. The wild wild Eastern Bloc would have me raped and killed and called out as a dirty Jew, like they used to, all for a woman who is nearly a stranger, an egg donor, pickled in the brain to be sure.

× × × ×

Ian Svenonius was the lead singer of the 1990s radical punk band Nation of Ulysses. He wrote the books *The Psychic Soviet* and *Supernatural Strategies for Making a Rock 'n' Roll Group*. He proclaimed that four is a magic number, a potent ingredient in the formation of a rock group. Svenonius is a Marxist from Washington, D.C., who views a four-person band as one of the few means of subversion available to oppressed peoples.

The Gang of Four were Chinese Communist Party officials who formed a treasonous group spearheading the Cultural Revolution led by Mao Zedong's last wife. She killed herself in 1991, while living out a life sentence in prison.

The year I was born, 1978, the band Gang of Four released their stark finger-pointer of a song called "Damaged Goods."

Four years later, four people sat together in a Leningrad apartment. They were comprised of four generations of firstborn girls, a nesting Matryoshka doll of a great-grandmother, a grandmother, a mother, and her daughter—tiny, last, solid wood inside.

The four-year-old girl watched from the bed she shared with the eldest one as the three women drank homemade vodka around a little square table covered with a waxed-canvas cloth. Her folks were about to get a divorce and the mother would lose her parental rights shortly thereafter.

In a town of three women there was a fourth. No one ever remembered to feed her, no one laid out clothes for her, no one bought new shoes for her, no one set aside a comb for her, no one looked for the lice in her hair, no one checked the scabs on her legs, *and yet in spite of all this she continued to live in the town without resenting what it did to her.* She considered herself a formidable candidate for their clique.

There are four forgotten saints in the Russian Orthodox Church—Faith, Hope, Charity, and their mother, Sophia-the-Martyr. The feast of these saints is in September, the month I was born.

In Russian, the names of these saints are Vera, Nadezhda, and Lyubov.

My great-grandmother's name is Nadezhda—it means "Hope." She prayed to an old copper-cornered icon of the four saints in a hidden makeshift altar while religion was still forbidden. She often told me the story of Faith, Hope, and Charity when she got loose by lunchtime as we buttered black bread by the bay window in her flat.

Russian Believers keep a "red corner" in their home devoted to worship. When a loved one dies they are to be bathed, dressed in white, belt cinched at the waist, a paper, flower, or cloth crown placed on their head, feet facing the *Krásnyj úgol*. The mourners then keep a wet rag by the window for forty days so that the spirit can come back to the holy corner to bathe and visit with the family.

Sophia was a widow who raised her three daughters as Christians during the Roman Empire. The four of them were ordered to make a sacrifice to the goddess Artemis. Sophia's daughters were tortured then executed before her eyes upon their refusal. She was allowed to bury them and mourned on their graves until her own death. For her solidarity with their suffering she was blessed as the fourth martyr along with Vera, Nadezhda, and Lyubov.

Shortly after we buried my great-granny Hope and her coffin was moved from the red corner, I developed rheumatic fever and my mother temporarily quit vodka to nurse my inflamed valves back to health. I recovered, and she stayed sick. It didn't stick for her.

Holy is the crown of hope that perches in clipped wings.

Within the chambers of the heart are four main valves that help the organ we believe to be responsible for feeling our loss and our joy relax and contract during each beat.

If one of these valves malfunctioned, the backflow of blood would drown us. They will open and close at the right time and press on in their journey no matter the pace until one gets blocked as a result of heart disease.

Christianity has several examples of four signifying Death, with the Four Horsemen of the Apocalypse and the Four Last Things.

The Chinese believe the number four to be the unluckiest number known to man, since it sounds like the Chinese word meaning "death." They avoid it at all costs and structure their families, their homes, and their businesses around the erasure of this number. Most buildings in China are designed without a marked fourth floor. There is still an actual fourth floor if you count the windows, but if no button was allowed for it on the elevator because the structure was renumbered, we can skip it, if only in our imagination.

Christians bring flowers to graves to let people know the dead are cared for and their resting place is tended to in their memory. Jews put rocks and pebbles on graves to reflect a similar sentiment.

VI

I absentmindedly picked at my petticoat netting under the blue velvet dress that I wore to ballet performances at the legendary Kirov Theatre. My dad would gently slap my hand when I lifted up the hem too high while fidgeting around next to him in our subway seats. He would give me a quick wink to say, *Sorry, kid, rules are rules.* The dress was made for me from scraps gleaned by my mother's friend who shared her namesake and was the costume designer for the Mariinsky Ballet Company. It had an adjustable waist sash and was to be worn as a floor-length gown in the beginning and eventually transition to a flouncy miniskirt number in the years to come.

Dad taught me how to open fancy chocolate wrappers without making a sound once we were in the red velvet chairs looking up at the gold-leaf ceiling and the botanical motifs carved into the balconies, like an inverted cake for a queen. The hunger kept me full. Artfully unveiling the candy was more delicious than letting it melt between the tongue and parched roof of my mouth.

At intermission we queued up for the little black caviar canapés, but only one each. I took mine away into the heat of the crowd in the lobby. I was there alone, in my version of a night at the theater. I walked around touching the protruding plaster angels in the hallway mirrors. My father misplaces and then finds me, not lost, but consumed by playing a woman on her own, proud, primping, wrist held high, nodding to passersby, needing no escort or assistance. No canned orchestra mothers to accompany me.

Back in our seats I imagined this was my living room and I had generously welcomed these strangers sitting behind me into my palace. Their faces looked so pleased in anticipation of the second act, so cozy, familiar, and warm—precisely planted together like a Christmas tree farm. I pined for her, a ground of brown needles, drippy with sap.

× × × ×

On top of his full-time college course load, Dad had a job fixing busted sinks and toilets at his school. He hid away his plumbing tools and wore a crisp white shirt to blend in with the other students who didn't perform menial labor to support a child, or in case he ran into cute girls. Gabriel also hustled up some seasonal work selling watermelons out of the back of a truck in the summer, and in winter, he was on to slinging pine trees sourced through clandestine methods. The man who hired him took a bunch of guys into the woods after dark to chop and load up whatever they could harvest in a hurry for as far as the reach of the headlights permitted. They would then park by the busiest train stations where ladies in woolen boots and fur hats paid a little extra to get the young men to haul their trees home for them.

There was no Christmas in the Soviet Union, officially. But we did get a holiday tree, religiously. We opened our presents on New Year's Day. Like most Russians, we had a plastic figurine of *Ded Moroz*, Old Man Frost, and his granddaughter, *Snegurochka*, the Snow Maiden, under our tree. A whole nation never wondering why this cold man was alone with this young girl whose job was to assist him in delivering the gift of winter. We all displayed a frozen child whose mother was all but out of the picture as our holiday centerpiece, conspiring in the myth that she is magically capable, diligent, selfless, and not lonely or creeped out by the old man.

That she is unmarred by seasons of obedience. That she likes to work for the man.

I do not recall a single New Year's Day when I woke up and you were there to open presents with me. I would go to bed staring up at the red star on the tree illuminating the yellow duck curtains in my dad's study, which doubled as my room in the beginning years, and think about the jolly old man's wife, whose figurine didn't exist, but her face floated around the room like I had been inhaling anesthetic gas, nevertheless. Swedish doctors have come up with a proper name for this withdrawn state—*uppgivenhetssyndrom*—resignation syndrome.

Refugee children with recent temporary asylum in Sweden, when told that they would not receive permanent residence, became catatonic and limply accepted feeding tubes from doctors who deemed them *de apatiska*, the apathetic. It was recorded that a typical refugee child in their care "lies completely still on the examination table and shows no reaction to caregiving. The doctor lifted Georgi's wrists a few inches above his forehead and then dropped them. 'They fall down on his face,' she wrote."

The observation notes on resignation syndrome in 2017, sound like hallucinations of motherlessness in 1987:

The patients have no underlying physical or neurological disease, but they seem to have lost the will to live.
I think it is a form of protection, this coma they are in.
They are like Snow White. They just fall away from the world.

Mothering is dictated by proximity, followed by a psychic absorption of the love object, so the closeness can be carried on anywhere regardless of distance. The inversion of this can never hold. Mothers who come back after loving from afar for any serious length of time will be gravely punished as they troll after their grown children with a warm scarf during winter, or a bowl of porridge in the haste of the morning. I still would like to try having her beg me to wipe my nose.

I want those first rights of refusal.

Refrigerator mothers were once held responsible for causing mental illness in their offspring. Their inadequate displays of affection disturbed the child into a disorganized and frenzied state. The fathers probably read this hypothesis in the newspaper they never looked up from long enough to notice their wives were legally drugged and stripped of purpose beyond enthusiastically cooing, "Open wide, darling, thaaaaaaaatah girl."

× × × ×

In the five years I came home from boarding school with a series of ailments, your ex-husband tried to be my sick nurse, to wean his inconsolable girl from needing a mother whose stilts he could no longer hack at to bring her back down to our level. After the mobile clinic doctor would leave shaking his head because I was too thin and my fever too high, Dad taught me to put a towel over my head and breathe in the steam from boiled potatoes to clear the sinuses, to grind up mustard seeds and tape the paste to the back of my neck when swollen lymph nodes wouldn't drain, to sip hot milk with a dollop of butter and a spoonful of honey, to rub vodka on a wheezing chest, to stuff garlic into wool socks to draw out impurities, to tightly wrap up in a camel hair blanket to shiver and sweat through the night.

He swabbed little glass jars with alcohol and lit them on fire, blowing them out and sticking the rims onto my back to make rows that left brown marks in a turtle-shell pattern.

I must have had delirium tremens by proxy, the way a partner might feel sympathy pains during labor. Somatization implies that our cells, our antigens and pathogens, are ruled and activated by the anxieties of the mind. But I had no body without you. The things that touched, the cups creating suction, the shots in my flat behind blooming with indigo rosebuds of scar tissue, all passed through me like in a lost-and-found bin at a bus depot. Nothing was mine to be absorbed because I wasn't absorbed by you, or you by me. I could buy the ticket, take the ride, but never arrive at my body, clean and fed. Not until I cleaned and fed children of my own.

VII

I gave birth to my daughter on 12/12/12, which equals 36, the age of my mother when she came over to my uncle's place and demanded to be given my address in America. Skeptical, he phoned his brother, who requested she continue to be kept in the dark as to our exact whereabouts. She was drunk, smelled bad, and needed a place to crash and sober up, so he gave her the four corners of his bed instead of a place to mail a letter, feeling guilty and saddened by her misfortunes.

I have asked my uncle Chanukah many times to tell me the story of my mother reaching out and being shunned without my permission. The part I can't seem to store away in my memory's lockbox is of him changing the bed after she is gone. He strips the dirty sheets like an orderly would at any hospital with patients checking in and checking out, dead or alive.

I would like to wear an equivalent of a medical alert bracelet: I lost my mother and I cannot find her—née Danilova.

My uncle is the oldest of four kids and is still a virgin. There is confusion over how he was given a diagnosis of schizophrenia, but one theory is that he suffered a head injury when his mother got hit by a car while carrying him. Chanukah managed to become an engineer and curate a floor-to-ceiling library ranging from *The Master and Margarita* to *The Count of Monte Cristo*—my main source of summer entertainment as a child.

He believes his mother, Chaya, was a saint even though she would not let him marry the only woman he deemed important enough to meet the family. I saw them parting outside a bookstore where she worked, and where he browsed almost every day instead of eating lunch, letting me tag along. He rested his forehead on her chest for a brief moment, trying to inhale her as they said goodbye. I never saw her again.

Breasts are four circles. The holes in those circles are countless.

Chanukah explained that when my mother couldn't care for me and stopped nursing me I was sent over to my granny's in Azerbaijan, where they took turns feeding and bathing me until my father had a better plan and brought me back home.

I was given mare's milk as a substitute. I was later assured that it contained more nourishment than my mother's ever could.

A weanling is a foal no longer feeding off the dam.

When mother winter arrived to collect her daughter after months of absence, so did the fevers that almost swallowed the baby. Did her presence cause the fevers or had mother winter come to cool her down? Chanukah says that an ambulance was called because they feared that my brain would be cooked. I had already begun walking and wouldn't come to my parents for comfort when they called me over with their wiggling fingers. At our reunion, my father commented that *her* child was now feral.

Horse mothers have sex with every stallion in the herd after they already know themselves to be pregnant. Since male horses have a territorial viciousness, this is the only way to confuse them into thinking that the foal may be theirs. The mare knows that if she fails to bed them all, one of the stallions will kick her foal around to death. Female horses have the ability to give themselves spontaneous abortions when this fate seems imminent for the gestating fetus.

Sometimes it feels like I sleep standing on all fours in a stable. Captured and whipped. Tamed and tired.

My mom told my father that her body was "too weak" to have an abortion in the Soviet system of no anesthetics and unsanitary, conveyer-belt-like conditions, and so he reluctantly agreed to let her keep me.

One of the first things I remember Luda teaching me is that we were both born in the Year of the Horse. She told me about the four elements and how they cycle through every twelve years in the Chinese calendar. Luda is a Fire Horse. I am an Earth Horse. Luda felt the damp spirit of my mother making my dirt darker and heavier, no matter how much she tried to warm me up with her light.

A foal that can't get up on all fours before the amniotic fluid dries on her fur is considered too sickly to stay alive. There is usually a heat lamp in the stable to help the babe find her way to the dam. To establish a bond, a wild horse marks the foal with her scent while licking her clean but follows the urge to gallop away with the herd if the little one has been touched by another mare, or is unhealthy.

I always thought that the word meaning *baby horse* was pronounced like the word *foul*—gross and smelly—but it's somewhere between the word *full* and the word *fall*.

Wholeness. Then void. Found. Then lost.

Say the word *foal* out loud.

VIII

It is hard to organize our days together in my congealed 1980s Soviet Union mind. The casualness of violence. The nearness of peril or harm like a dull click of an abacus. The decade is a bronze disease patina, the green paste, on a doorbell that rings when you show up, and you do not show up very often. When you do appear, the flip-book banalities marry the destruction in a figure eight of a skater tracing the ice in reverse at a reckless speed.

You sit in the bath facing me, not yet in your thirties. Your breasts used to be my breasts, belonged to me, would get too full and ache without me. Later, much later, when they have fed two mouths that have rarely spoken your name, mine look like what I once inhaled of a wandering mother—your dark blue veins, wet worms on cracked white tile. Like you, my body would become a lopsided provider, the muteness of the right breast forcing the left side to overfunction, to nearly explode with nurturing, with twice the volume. A drought and drown chest.

You tell me about your see-through skin, your thin-skinness. "Have you seen the paintings of noble ladies in the Hermitage?" you wonder aloud. If I look closely, their corseted, plump, and powdered bosoms have the same trolley rail lines that refuse to hide beneath the first light coating of Leningrad snow as your chest does. My father took me to museums, ballets, and operas almost every weekend, so you were asking a concrete, pointed question. Even though your family had lived in the most culturally rich city in Russia for generations, you never went to the Hermitage with your daughter—too much of a townie to act like a tourist on your native soil.

You stand up, a floating iceberg in the fog followed by your little girl's steam, and begin to dry off. Our ancestors come from good stock, you remind me. My breasts will surely turn out fine and delicate like yours. My blood will suck up the lost riches and formal tea times you imagine your ghosts once had and make a map on my body as well, unable to hide our true-blue ties.

We are in the four-by-four pea soup–green room with a toilet and torn-up newspapers at your feet that we wipe ourselves with when the tissue paper runs out. The smudged traces of *the truth* in the news. The smearing. The tainting of the facts. Flushed evidence.

It's my turn to go and you hoist me up onto the cold porcelain and read from the scraps you move around with your big toe, smoking a cigarette. I'm constipated, and you give me a puff of your smoke because it always helps you go. This trick works. I cough and open up and feel relief.

All of my holes feel different after this.

× × × ×

You argue with my dad over whether you are drunk again or not. He calls you a liar and you snap like hollow timber. My fingers squeeze the unvarnished wood of my toddler bed. I hear your ribs break as I press my face against the crib slats, which now shake like telephone wires in a hailstorm.

× × × ×

I watch you burn my milk, your face greasing the kitchen linoleum, robe over the waist, empty baby bottle in hand, brown rubber nipple still on the counter. I paw and knead your body like a blind kitten. The screams get our neighbor, Elizabeta Mikhailovna, to come out of her room in our communal flat and lead me away from the kitchen to watch her little black-and-white TV and suck on hot tea-soaked sugar cubes.

× × × ×

You wake me up in the middle of the night, probably drunk but happy, and insist we go out picking flowers. You get me dressed and we enter the warm, dusky light. The city is silent. We prowl the parks with the best landscaping, the ones with statues of a cast-iron Peter the Great mounting a horse or a granite Lenin bust squinting thoughtfully. We pluck branches and blooms as though harvesting our own private garden. I fall asleep blanketed in sweet pollen and petals. When I wake up, every surface of the room holds a container with lilacs, tulips, and hyacinths spilling out like bowing servants. You draped over your gaps and absences in this stolen beauty.

× × × ×

You have a few friends over. They say that they are in love and their teeth are wet and huge as they speak into each other's foreheads. You hug them tight and announce that you could marry them right now. You stumble over to the kitchen and get two dry green peas and sit in front of the couple you placed on the edge of your bed with wineglasses in their hands. "Let your love grow for each other like these peas sprouting in your bellies," you say, kneeling down in front of them, looking up into their red faces with now-heavy eyelids. You cross yourself and plop the peas into the liquor they take down with one gulp. I clap, and you look awake again.

I learn about filling a vessel in the dark—to not disturb your high with the turn of a light switch. Listen for the sound approaching the top. You will know when. You will know full if you fill enough cups in the dark. In your cups, girl.

Fun. Fun with problems. Problems. The mother of all problems. Mother problems are inherent multipliers. Your party-girl fissures reveal the hot lava spilling over as it burns captivated onlookers alive—mummifies, envelopes, seals up their every opening.

× × × ×

You are *asleep* on your side. An hour ago, it was dark in this room. Now all of the men you brought over have left. Thirty minutes ago, there was light. Granny Galina bravely chased them out of her bedroom. The one guy who was passed out in the chair with his flaccid dick sticking out of his pants was slow to move. Two hours ago, he told me it was a lollipop and I should taste it. He tried to grab my head after I flipped the light switch on to check up on you, but I ducked past him and wriggled out. The other two men cradling you from each side act like they don't see me. I step over spread-out legs, like blackberry brambles curled up in a ditch, and go call your mother on the hallway telephone. The other numbers I know to dial are 02 for the police, 03 for the ambulance, and 04 for the gas service.

When the lights are on for the last time the moaning stops and Granny gets to work, expertly escorting out the naked assembly, much too calmly for my taste. Her elbow moves up and down in an effort to scrub your period blood off her shiny sky-blue comforter once it's just us girls again. She mumbles about you "ruining her nice things" and gently pushes you over to get at more of the hot-pink stain. I turn out the lights. I am never left alone with you on purpose after this night.

IX

Each time I hold two of the most popular books written by French women, coincidentally about sex, masochism, sadism, and seeking oblivion, I instinctively imagine every turn of the page as a blanket for my mother's body, so riddled with shame. *Story of O* and *The Sexual Life of Catherine M.* are about giving power away and asserting power, but both through being taken, used, pounded, trashed, worshiped, entered. O dies. M lives.

The fact that the universal hole of *O* and the double-house schema of *M*, representing Mother, are conjoined here doesn't surprise me. I have seen the MOM in my SOS when calling for you. You are gaping, open wide, closed, and remote, all at once.

The movie made from the Pauline Réage book about O, forced to live in a castle where she is whipped and used by men in order to become a more loyal and devoted lover to her man, was a favorite bootlegged VHS tape procured by my father. Much like with *M*, *O* was about loss of control, curiosity, freedom, and numbers. Above all, volume. There was to be structure and order within the chaos—the first rule of proper mothering.

Pauline Réage is a name of the pen. Anne Cécile Desclos had a couple pseudonyms for publishing her love letters to seduce Jean Paulhan. Her object of desire even writes her a preface, entitled "Happiness in Slavery," purporting he has no clue who is the real author of the *Story of O*.

Some women aren't to be canonized, publicly accepted, or even acknowledged. My biggest fear as the missing daughter of an unseen and unheard mother pointed to the looming victim legacy as mine to surgically remove and dissect. Because everything started as a copy.

Catherine Millet only abbreviates her name in the title but carries no shame, no need for an empathetic relationship with her audience, no interest in being absorbed, revered, and mostly, no interest in being dominated—just penetrated. Millet is an unmother.

Some women's insides cannot betray their outsides even though the art they made was splendid, certainly more deserving of the attention Henry Miller basked in while he took Anaïs Nin's money. As every library became my foster home and every book a coded path to grappling with the absent woman who never actually raised me, just haunted me, a book like *Henry and June* roasted my throat with the fear that tough and smart doesn't protect you from subservient and used up.

I knew that Anaïs Nin was hot for Henry Miller and kept a journal about their trysts. Henry would say stuff like: "You drive me crazy with passion" and "Come here at once, it will be beautiful, I promise." Men like that—hungry, casually greedy, always landing on their feet while uttering the most clichéd things—were all around me. I hated that the woman I admired gave in to a bad romance, but since Anaïs was the closest comparison to both damaged and regal I could find, she was therefore the embodiment of Elena on a pedestal and in the gutter of my imagination.

I became very old once I saw those men having sex with her limp body. I became her mother and she my baby. Now, shaken, we were both crushed-ice girls, all mixed up. I would have to learn about Elena by reading an instructional manual that didn't exist. There were no chapters in novels or essays in anthologies that could teach me to keep loving Elena through witnessing what seemed like rape, but could have been a choreographed orgy, or even sex work. A choice, not choice.

So, I read about how Henry Miller entered Anaïs without needing any Vaseline, the way she did with her husband, and how her pussy was constantly wet for him. She was very busy mopping the slippery floors from their heat, and putting together little pastry trays for Henry to sustain him through inebriated writing sessions. She could have just made a weekly appointment with a dominatrix after her big business meetings, like the powerful men who control things in the big bad world would do. I guess you can't pay some guys to beat women when they'll do it for free.

Anaïs was supreme at her craft but was labeled a lying, neurotic, erotic diarist, which is something like being called a supercreative cleaning lady, if you ask me.

She was stapling her ripped-open knees to kitchen floors, waiting for her top-shelf treat, because hers and Henry's passion was worth being cut down to size, where she was already small, in the SOS parts below, where her dad used to give her the most attention.

Henry Miller is a fantastic professional loser, a foreshadowing of male slacker culture. Using your gorgeous young wife for inspiration is great genius to be sure. June was moving his pen with her damn cunt. I wish I were kidding, but it's just not that funny. I think she might have been distracted, like, the entire time. Even her muse of a cunt couldn't get his horny verse to compost, because Anaïs was stealing away all the heat and melting the Vaseline inside until the lines blurred.

Unlike June, Anaïs didn't actually need him, because she had all the money from her genial husband and was not gonna die on the side of the road when they were done mating like dogs. Anaïs died in luxury as more than just Henry Miller's fuck-buddy-pen-pal-cruisin'-for-a-bruisin' and that is a legacy all its own. Certainly a brighter ending than my mother's, once her husband found a younger woman and, later, a ticket to crawl out from beneath the Iron Curtain without a goodbye.

X

In Soviet times, Russian babies were bound in tight swaddles for the first four months of their helpless existence. The hospitals, understaffed and lacking in medical equipment, relied on ancient methods of soothing. The babies in a maternity ward were placed against a wall in their cocoons and were not tended to until they became irate or the schedule allowed for it.

Bondage is believed by some scientists to reduce anxiety. Submissives refer to this bliss of restraint, this freedom of captivity, as "rope space."

Once pregnant, a woman faces four outcomes. Abortion. Miscarriage. Live delivery. Stillborn delivery.

Everything after that is a process of adding or subtracting to reach zero. You are not asked, but told, to give in.

And then if you are not feeding, you are bleeding.

× × × ×

Hall of Fame. Hall of Shame. That's motherhood—from the maternity ward, where a sweet and patient nurse forces you to walk and to pee on your own, then helps put on your stretchy hospital underwear and pad, to the passing fanfare back home where the phone stops ringing, replacing questions about your day with screams and vomit. The violent shaking and puking in the transition stage of labor will cycle through your post-birth world with no hair-of-the-dog cures to relieve you. Physical autonomy and libidinal discharge live apart now, marooned on distant shores.

Why can't it be both ways? Why do mothers have to be forgotten or brave, like soldiers? Why must the telling be the sensational center, and not the sentence, not the craft, not the gestation of words?

I get to feel truly lonely, but never alone, when I become a mother for the first time, a month before my thirtieth birthday. Maybe that's the whole point of conception. When offered only commas and ellipses you will bust your tail to find a period; a full stop. Then the train never comes, and you wonder how to get home. You went to your old train stop like a fool and it is now permanently under construction.

One day, long before she gives birth, a girl might reach down in the shower after fourth period to find that she is *a woman* and zombie walk to all the frightened girls in her gym class and scream out that she is dying. She must be dying. They will close their eyes, push, spit, and shout, like at a sold-out concert. They will throw giant pads at her as she tries to hug their repulsed, stiff bodies, their clean cotton shirts smelling of name-brand detergent and mothers who mop their white kitchen tiles every day and teach them to wash down there just as seamlessly as their own mothers once did.

Carrie's mother knew where the tragedy began, the SOS of her daughter. I have almost given up hope that I might acquire cunt telekinesis one of these days. So, I remain a faithful ballbuster instead.

× × × ×

When I was little I spent nights thinking about choice as though I were a witch. What would I choose if I had to pick from a set of things? I chose by looking at the see no evil, hear no evil, speak no evil monkey figurine my father kept on his desk along with a paperweight of the Romulus and Remus twins suckling a she-wolf.

I thought that you have to know, even if there is no choice, which would you rather be? Are you afraid of the dark, child? Are you in love with music, girl? Are you trying to tell me something, baby? I tossed these around and, too often fearing the loss of eyesight and hearing, always caught the mute ball.

If God had stricken me with one of these at birth, or if there were a war and I had the choice between a bomb going off near my house, the explosion rupturing my eardrums, or the shrapnel going in my eyes, I wished for neither. I would then have to get tortured, my tongue cut off by the enemy soldiers who invaded Russia in my recurring fear during the Cold War. I was relieved to think I would become permanently inarticulate and never tell stories I was not allowed to tell anyway, because the woman of risk and suffocating candor who made this mouth was always unspeakable.

I think that the see no evil, hear no evil, speak no evil monkey needs a fourth set of arms to cover her crotch.

When I was about eight my mother gave me an unsolicited sex talk. As she dried off after a bath I asked her whether I would grow a mound of pubic hair like hers. I was a child with much fuzz in embarrassing places, like the nape of my neck, lower back, and to my horror, my vagina. Soon I would be nothing but fur, like her wild fur, but worse. She tilted her head sideways and asked me if I knew that she took my father's virginity. She made a cup out of her hand, as though scooping water from an invisible fountain. It was my fa-

ther's long-gone balls she was miming for me; a terrifying performance. She was once a powerful teacher and held court over his
young body before she was escorted stage right with divorce-paper
confetti in the air. My eventual stepmother was handed the broom
so no trace of her ticker-tape parade out of our lives would remain.

XI

Leningrad is made up of more than forty islands on the delta of the river Neva. It has a rainy maritime climate in fall and spring. The river freezes over completely in the winter, connecting the islands below as they are by the bridges above. In the summer it is a musky, humid swamp. Between all the rain, the snow, the fog, the freezes, and the thaws, the city, which has one of the greatest art collections in the world, is constantly fighting off the erosion of such pervasive dampness.

The Hermitage museum is like a glacier—we see only the peaks. What's underneath is simply too massive to navigate. The secrets that are stacked away in the museum's storage facilities are vast. And so are the lies to cover them up, like the known fakes they can't admit to, or the poorly executed restorations that have to be accepted, or the German paintings that were looted by the Red Army, held captive until they were finally exhibited, but not given back to their proper owners, those most original of enemies.

There is a famous Soviet-era film, the name of which I forget now, that deals with the sadistic elements of coveting an embroidered lifestyle within the spartan and spare Soviet commitment to *equality*. In it, a woman who shares a communal space with a true daughter of the revolution gets a lesson about flying too high, her shiny earrings ripped out as she lifts her leg to roll up her silk stockings. The message is if you flaunt it, we got it, and you ain't getting it back. Mother Russia is above parents, above religion, and definitely above Self.

Maybe only poetry can compete for first place in the Russian black bread heart. Think of what Lenin asked the peasants to do—to storm the palace and kill the Tsar—to move into his house, confiscate his prized possessions, and, theoretically, to oversee the redistribution of wealth. Most important, to restage the royal whimsies and heirlooms as a public museum, an ongoing humiliation, a warning to anyone who had once participated in amassing a fortune or openly strived to do so in the future. A synchronized coveting was to be our utmost indulgence. Unlike the new Russia of ostentatiousness without irony. The invisible banners these days seem to read: NOW, WITH PALACES FOR SOME.

During the Siege of Leningrad, Stalin decided to starve the people but save the art. The museum and archival staff took down the ancient statues from their pedestals and carefully wrapped them in burlap or whatever cloth they could find. Some families did not have enough wood both to make coffins for children who died of hunger and to keep the living warm, even after all of the furniture was broken down and burned for heat, after cherished books of poems were used as kindling.

Those who lived in the basement of the Hermitage, looking after the dead-eyed busts of Medusa and building frames around the billowy capes of Mercury, ate chalk and glue and stayed cold at night while these artworks without actual wants—empty guts, phlegmy lungs, slowing pulses—were as cozy and cocooned as newborn babies.

Fourteen years after the brutal conclusion of the Leningrad Blockade, "the stubbornness that possibly led to more deaths than surrender may have," Great-Granny Hope used to tell me—Gentile to Jew, you were born in the same hospital where you would later give birth to me. The same pea soup–green walls of our bathroom, a popular Soviet-era color, were now peeling around the doorframes in the 1970s. Another reminder that restorations do not last; that erosion and loss are inevitable; that intentions do not prepare us for the sacrifices of actual doing; that walls are like people, either tended to, primed and coated in something shiny and new by the beloved, or left to crumble toward the abyss.

XII

Pushkin is a quaint little suburb of Leningrad where I attended an Internat—a specialized tuition-free boarding school that was a mixed bag of locals who used it as a day school, kids who went home to Leningrad on the weekends and whose parents could pop in any time since the school was only an hour and a half away, as well as orphans and temporary wards of the state with caring grandparents and social workers who used the socialized education system to get them an interview for a sought-after spot. The town was the first to acquire a rail service when it was the Tsar's Village and the last residence of the dethroned blue bloods, later dedicated to the memory of the country's favorite poet, a descendant of a slave who became a nobleman. Pushkin's languid ponds and gardens aren't very far from the grand summer palaces of the village of Peterhof—once similarly plundered by the Germans—where an intricate hydraulic system was installed to power marvelous fountains so the Imperial clan could cool off in the summer and find solace from the metronome of the city.

My boarding school had wrought iron beds, den mothers, knitting, ballet, violin lessons, cross-country skiing to get around, sketching ruins al fresco, wild strawberries in the woods picked under nets, snowdrops and lilies-of-the-valley, shoe covers on museum tours, oak leaf piles, hiding wet sheets, and running away to my mother's place.

I was to live here from first until fifth grades and come home on the weekends and holidays only so that my dad, who had also attended boarding school, wouldn't have to worry about bad kids or predators in the neighborhood, about feeding me dinner every night on a tight budget, and about my mother showing up at the house breathing out ethanol and telling unseemly stories to her latchkey daughter. I was expected to get the hang of the commute early on so that my father didn't waste three hours of his Monday mornings to drop me off.

When I tell my father I am upset that everyone teases me at boarding school and around Pushkin because my butt shows if I lift my arms up in the air, he responds by getting me a new uniform four sizes too big. The year I began noticing boys I looked like they shrunk the school lunch lady.

He bought me white ribbed tights for special days and brown ribbed ones for every day, which were all a few sizes up to avoid standing in lines more than necessary. He put my future clothes under his bed. One day before the May Day parade he pulled out a plastic bag and struggled to put my good, white ribbed tights on me. I had grown, but he hadn't noticed. So I walked with the crotch way too low on my thighs. It was hard to sit on his shoulders to see the procession of tanks and floats when I couldn't spread myself wide enough to hold on.

A lesson to hug with my legs when I'm all grown up.

× × × ×

Our national regulation school uniforms were wool blends of chocolate brown. The aprons worn over the dresses were black for every day and white pinafores for special occasions. Our white collars and cuffs were to be removed with tiny scissors, washed, starched, ironed, and sewn back on every weekend at home.

Nothing and no one was allowed to stand out or be special. There were, maybe, two types of toothpaste, but there was no branding, no pictures to indicate a flavor. Toothpaste was medicinal—it served a clinical purpose to protect teeth from rot. Children in commercials did not delight in products that enticed them with ads. There was no bubble bath shaped like a cartoon character. There were no superhero toothbrushes. There was no good or bad soap. There's just soap you use for hand-washing of clothes and soap you use on your body, usually once a week for both.

Laundry and bathing were events. In boarding school, we were taught what I remember as the face-pits-and-crotch mini sink baths. You were basically encouraged to scrub your face and rinse under your arms as fast as possible due to the unpredictable availability of hot water, and for menstruating girls, to wash *down there*. Unlike at the Internat, most people went to *banyas*, the communal steam rooms, to bathe properly by sweating the week off and getting a lashing with bundled oak leaves in soapy water rather than waiting on the shared tub in their flat. The communal aspect of everything, down to something personal, like hygiene, was to be cooperative; beaten and bathed into us as Soviets.

One of the girls in my dorm had orange-flavored toothpaste imported from Poland, and I would wait for her to go to sleep and sneak it out of her nightstand to carefully squeeze some onto my own toothbrush. It tasted like creamy chalk with citrus rind, and I slowly ate it in little cat-licks. I ended up sucking on the other girls' toothpastes, too. Mine was powder, which was cheapest and had no added flavor to it.

I would steal black bread that the other kids left behind on the tables after a dinner of kasha and stuffed cabbage and save it in the front pockets of my apron. I would lay out these scraps on the giant cast-iron heaters in our room of twenty squeaky beds lined up against bare walls and let them toast up for snacks of croutons we called *syuchari*.

In third grade I learned that my teacher expected sugar. Tamara Ye-stafyevna certainly enjoyed a few lumps in her tea, but she also made sweet water, which she used to wash her blackboard. This made the chalk appear more vivid, gave it more traction, I suppose. Her board was actually brown and gleamed like a mirror. If you brought her a kilo you got on her good side. Our rations could never be stretched that far, and nothing could buy me out of hot ears on the way to the principal's office or being called the smelly girl anyhow. She decided to not take down a pencil-colored poster that was obviously made by my classmates and casually appeared on the community board. In it, I was depicted on a pee bed, yellow ring, hair disheveled, and squiggly fumes emanating from all sides.

My teacher's most productive punitive measure was to make us all stand next to our desks with arms stretched forward until whoever stole an object off her desk or did some other sneaky thing would confess. We had to collectively hate mysteries, learn to tattle for the greater good, be advanced sleuths, and suspect everyone of wrong-doing in the process. Sometimes no one would confess, and she was forced to let us go once the bell rang. I always wondered if it was me who was supposed to confess, if I had imagined being innocent, and rubbed my arms on the way to a mirror in the basement mud-room where everyone pulled on their boots for outdoor recess. I never asked the mirror if I was the transgressor. I took out my hidden chocolate and warmed it against my lips, pretending it was the brown lipstick my mother wore. I puckered and blended, then licked it off so no one would see me this way.

XIII

The inside of black bread is moist, acidic, and clay-like. The crust is coarse, the top of the brick shape is practically charred, and the rest is a copper brown. It's cheaper than white bread, about twenty kopecks for a whole loaf. When I'm home, my job is to buy the milk and the bread. There are always lines and they are quite dull. The shopkeepers are never happy to see you and appear interchangeably exhausted and lazy.

At the dairy store, my two white galvanized pitchers get filled up from a giant vat of whole milk by a greasy tin ladle. The lids never stay shut on my containers and the milk spills fat, cloudy raindrops all over my tan legs, the wooden handles soaking with sweat.

Both the bakery and the dairy are just a few blocks down busy Bronnitskaya Street, where I grew up in a five-story ornate yellow stucco apartment building with frozen drainpipes and icicles menacingly dripping from green cornices. The rows of apartment buildings are all broken up by archways leading out into the shared courtyards I mostly avoided after losing touch with the neighborhood kids once I began first grade in Pushkin. Sitting on my windowsill, I would watch them and make little thimble-size cups out of the doughy part of the black bread. I roll chunks of the inner flesh into balls and press my index finger inside to make a mold that will resemble a vessel. Once I have four or five of these, I pour in the milk, barely a sip in each, and swallow them whole one by one, the milk popping inside the salty fake china I sculpted.

My father was honest with me about our lack of money, lack of food. We'd sit at our narrow kitchen table pushed up against the left-side wall, same as our neighbors had staged theirs, with the single window looking out over the courtyard, and talk about division and fairness.

"We have only this one piece of sausage," he'd say.

In between us, on the table that our state-assigned flatmates don't share, because they take their food into their rooms, is a white plate with a kielbasa, some mustard, a hunk of black bread, and a knife.

"I'm hungry. Do I get to eat it now?"

"It's up to you."

"Why is it in the middle like that?"

"Well, because you have to make a choice, like a mature person."

"Can I have my own sausage, please?"

"This is all we got for now until I get paid again. You can take the knife and split it however you see fit. I can either stay hungry myself and watch you eat the whole thing, or we can do as God taught us, and share."

"But then we will both still be hungry."

"Less so. We feel our joys and our pains together. We share, to ease the burden."

"Do we have any milk left?"

Realizing I can fill up on milk, I cut the kielbasa in half and give my father the piece that looks biggest, even if the difference is too slight to really notice. When we are done eating, my father gives me a kiss on the head and tells me to do the dishes.

× × × ×

I was a clumsy child. As I sneak more food, I drop a big jar of jam and it breaks, but only around the rim. I thought that all the slivers and shards were accounted for, picked out, but as I ate the preserved strawberries I felt myself accidentally swallow something sharp and hard. I sat on the balcony and faced the sun, preparing myself for death. I wouldn't make it to fourth grade, use the microscope in botany class, shape marzipan out of almond paste, paint it with beet and carrot juice, and dip it in sugar until it looked like a peach.

I wouldn't share a sweet kiss at an open-air cinema with a boy who reminds me of Lermontov.

I assumed the shard would find its way to my heart, like a wet body down a swift and winding tube at a water park. I stared past the sun as it baked my forehead, nearsighted and without glasses. When nothing happens, I go back inside and tell no one about the visions of my demise, or the danger in the jar. I don't throw away the preserves, but I don't touch them again.

Later, my father threw a sedate party. Splayed out on the couch across a tightly packed line of my father's dear friends from school, I wore a terry cloth jumper with big buttons on the front. The lady in a pencil skirt brought me a banana, a rare tropical treat, which I ate bit by bit, teeth scraping the fibrous, gum-numbing peel once the flesh is consumed. One of the women had my head in her lap, another had her arms wrapped around my torso, and the third played with my slippers—all impromptu babysitters who asked me with delight and sincerity about my scrambled-egg recipe and snuck me chocolates.

Before passing out, I read *Pippi Longstocking*, one leg swung over another to prop up the book, which I plucked from my uncle's cavernous library. Pippi made up stories about her absent parents' fantastical adventures: the father who was a brave captain of a ship and vanished at sea after a storm but would surely be back, and an angel mother whom Pippi did not remember but who reassured her, while Pippi was looking up at the sky, that she would be all right alone in the world. Like Pippi, I liked to pretend that my mother was watching over me, that she and my father had a higher calling in life—I imagined her as a great painter and him as a tortured poet—that they were benevolent creatures, remote and mysterious in order to serve a larger purpose for society.

Maybe children aren't always children. Maybe it's up to the adults to keep them so.

XIV

If your mother won't stand behind you brushing your hair, saying—
Look how beautiful you are, I'm so proud of you, don't listen to a
word those other miserable lost souls say, I know who you are, my
strong, my brave, my lovely little girl, you're nobody's punching bag,
God don't make no junk and you're my jewel of a prize who I waited
for all my life—you get to choose whatever you feel like wearing no
matter the price.

There were so many versions of this motherly love mantra I had told
myself in the mirror as a small child braiding my hair every morning. I'd wake up extra early determined to French braid my dirty

and unbrushed locks—black, crunchy, and greasy—into something that I could rescue while hiding the fact that I had no one to get me ready for school, no one to make me take a bath on Sunday nights.

As a girl, being unkempt and smelly as I was in my neglected state was a sin that boys got away with all the time. I braided my hair to protect my family and the dignity I believed was my duty to preserve until my arms fell asleep, until I made myself late for school.

I wouldn't dare wake up my dad and any overnight guests he may have had, so I looked through their coats for the money I needed to get to school. If I couldn't find enough I would panhandle. My strategy was to stand by the change machines at the subway turn-stile and cry.

Eventually someone would notice a little girl in a school uniform weeping alone and came over to ask me what had happened to upset me. I would say that the machine ate my money and I'm desperately late for class. Most of the time I would get more than my fare.

Rush hour down the subway escalator is like an avalanche, a con-trolled explosion on the slopes. A tiny kid with a violin case, a back-pack full of finished homework, and a sack of clean laundry she had scrubbed and dried on the line for the week ahead could get swal-lowed up. At times all I could see were people's belts and crotches, behinds and hips, squishing me until the opening above almost closed up; until I couldn't breathe and yell out for help, help down there, beneath being seen.

I ran away from boarding school and walked around looking for my mother instead of attending violin lessons. I skipped lessons regularly and lied about it to my father, who was jittery with shame after my recitals, signaling a future beating would take place behind closed doors with a smack upside the head. The unspoken rule was that if I didn't use them to listen and play the notes, my ears were to be boxed. Most of the time I said goodbye to my boarding school teachers, waving my sheet music and my violin case at them, and walked around Pushkin kicking icicles out of drainpipes or watching people shop for dinner at the bazaar.

I was going to trap her into taking care of me, as though she just needed a reminder, as though she were simply having a bad day year after year and had forgotten how to move her hands from her closed eyes. I must have thought she would cry out with relief and tell me how exhausted she was from running around trying to get me back, how smart I was to read her mind and come to her at once. What sore eyes you have, mother dear.

Some freezing day in second grade I got off at her subway stop like a dog going on instinct. I walked over to her building complex and stood in the courtyard, shouting up at the gray concrete facades. I tried to search out her windows, but they were all the same. The dark squares looked like gaping mouths screaming back at me.

I want you to stand out in the cold and pine for my windows to open, Mother.

XV

I met my future stepmother for the first time in a Leningrad subway station when I was in second grade. Luda was a twenty-year-old
transplant from a small Ukrainian town, painted with shiny scarlet
lipstick and heavy eyeliner, prowling for adventure and male gener-
osity. Instead of finding easy fun, she got hit on by a single father
in a fake fur coat, thirty-five kopecks in his pocket and an empty
fridge in a communal flat. She soon discovered he was a Jew from
the Caucus region, which solidified his endearing outsider status
and confirmed that she had not hit the suitor jackpot, but since he
was less of a drifter than she was, it didn't matter.

For his and Luda's first date, Dad hand-sewed a pair of black velvet bell-bottoms and designed a pullover with billowing sleeves and white piping to match. He worshiped the Beatles and managed to create outfits from scratch based on their well-cataloged changing tastes. He sat in a chair facing a wall at a short enough distance to make his shoes curl up in the front because he saw in a magazine that the Beatles wore ankle boots that didn't lay flat at the tips. He had photos of Jean-Paul Belmondo and Marcello Mastroianni on his bedroom wall. He took self-portraits that he printed and developed in our bathroom. In the black-and-white photos, he wears a striped V-necked sweater and a fedora, cocked sideways atop his mop of black waves. His mouth is slightly parted, and he holds up his chin with a fanned-out hand, like Rimbaud.

Once my mother lost her parental rights and moved back in with my granny, I was to be raised by a man who was trying to put some miles between him and his draining divorce. Gabriel was in love with every woman he ever bedded, it seemed. He was promiscuous, but he would never be called a slut, and he didn't become a social outcast because he couldn't commit to any one lady. I try to lie to the women he is seeing about his fidelity, his whereabouts, his intentions. I can't keep all their names straight.

But how I loved all of the grown-ups' fossils; the remnants left behind by my dad's ladies. I cleaned up after them so that his sort-of full-time girlfriend, who became my stepmother, didn't find other women's underwear, photographs, handwritten notes, and clumps of hair in the drain.

One time I couldn't keep a story straight and it led to Luda coming home to confront one of the other women. She came into the kitchen where I was eating alongside my dad and this random mistress, who wore Luda's house slippers and housecoat. She saw the slipper dangling on this lady's foot as she nervously shook her crossed leg back and forth. "You slut!" Luda screamed, and kicked the shoe off the woman's foot so hard it somersaulted in the air and landed by the window about eight feet away.

Luda charged at her and began ripping the robe off her body. The lady wore nothing underneath. I had been trying her on for size to fit into the many compartments of my mother-wanting imagination. It was jarring to see this would-be caretaker fighting and losing her dignity in front of my dad. It was a girl fight. A tired, old, dime-a-dozen kind of fight over a man, going all the way back to when they both had to leave their childhood to be courted or ignored. Girl competition can be refereed easily. The slut will never win. She has no credibility. She gets no points. A group decides who the slut is by singling her out, kicking her out of the tribe. Once she gets the smell of the competition out, Luda will wear her robe again in a sad triumph.

× × × ×

Luda was a seamstress. Her mother ran a garment factory and taught her how to operate a sewing machine at an early age. My father convinced Luda to move in, and soon after, he helped her buy an industrial-size sewing machine so that she could work from home. When she left the house on errands, I immediately sat behind her sewing table and began turning out my own projects. I managed to break the machine almost every time. When she got back and asked me why the needle had snapped off or the thread was tangled up in the bobbin, I shrugged and refused to admit to any wrongdoing. I thought that her return home was the biggest inconvenience. I was practicing being the lady of the house—I was lost playing mother.

A sewing machine is like a mother bent over, cradling her pregnant belly, with the round bobbin inside firmly attached: moving, beating, fluttering, and spinning out a new life. I spent long stretches of time sewing what I imagined were perfect garments only to find out that the bobbin had run out of thread a long time ago. The ghost stitch on top was useless on its own; it didn't hold without the bottom stitch. The bobbin is much like the uterus, holding a baby of new silky thread. It demands ongoing repair and replenishment; its umbilical cord pokes out to connect with the needle above.

The summer before I turned nine I fantasized about having a sewing machine of my very own. In June, during the white nights, the whole city of Leningrad was drunk on the heavy scent of blooming lilacs; the boozy light of a never-dark sky seemed to liquefy all the purple bushes in the squares like Vaseline on a camera lens. The gauze of endless daylight and that bright perfume in the air kept me up at night, staring out of my wide-open windows and eventually falling asleep satisfied by the vision of a little companion sewing machine to the one my stepmother used.

In September, the Iron Curtain parted temporarily for my ninth birthday. I received a plastic German sewing machine from my father and Luda. They surely pulled strings to procure it during the Soviet era of black-market dealings. I became preoccupied with stitching things together: anything, even paper at first. When a friend would come over and try to tell me a story or play with me, I ignored her; all of her words were muffled and spun through the whir of my motor and foot pedal furiously plowing through projects. I was making contact, willing things to go together, marrying shapes and creating everything and nothing.

× × × ×

When Luda first came into our lives she was four months pregnant with twins by a nameless man from her previous relationship. I was in second grade and slept with wet braids so that my boring stick-straight hair could be curly on the weekends. Luda said it made me look like a little wild monkey and did her best to groom me into a girl-child, but I mostly wanted to be in the animal kingdom.

I trapped mice in jars at my boarding school and took them on the train ride back to Leningrad with me. If it was a nice day I entertained my captives, opening up the tall casement windows facing a busy street and singing with my arms stretched out, like I had seen the abundantly painted ladies perform their arias at the theater with my father. I also dragged dingy alley cats on my way back home from the park and begged Luda to adopt them. Somehow, she allowed this as long as the new feral pet could be cleaned up.

We would tie cloth around their paws to protect us from their gray, curved claws and soap them up as they wailed and writhed in the tub. When one of her favorite strays managed to escape as I left for school one morning, Luda thought that I had stolen her for myself, as a secret pet to keep in my dormitory. Decades later, she still doesn't believe that this cat could not be domesticated, that she left willingly.

Luda miscarried the twins a few weeks after moving in, right on my dad's bed. Strange women hovered around her as she cried. One of them gave her a shot that made her contorted face go slack.

I stayed behind, wiping her forehead with a cold towel by the light of a darkroom lamp. Red on. Red off. The room is full. The room is empty. And so this woman is to be reminded each month after month from then on.

× × × ×

My father started shooting and printing photographs once Luda settled in. He got an enlarger and periodically set up our communal bathtub as his darkroom. He strung up a rope with clothespins that pinched the corners of pictures in which they posed for the camera, she in a G-string and he in a tight tank top and bow tie. When I looked at them, repulsed and intrigued by their games, they seemed shy and amazed at themselves for being so brazen, breathless from barely running ahead of the self-timer.

XVI

Born in January 1956, Elena was a true Russian winter mother—
you'll never know how bad she'll be, or when she's coming or going.
January is about exiting the longest night of the winter equinox.
Darkness almost all day. Opposite of the white nights of a Leningrad
summer.

She still shines to me when I'm that kid, chest-deep in virgin snow
on my way to the subway station, black morning sky, little body
drawing a map like a caterpillar crunching forward on a pale leaf.

Mother winter is all surface beauty. Want to lick her like buttercream icing, like glistening egg whites beaten for a birthday cake. But cold slows us down and makes us sleepy until we are high and hallucinating, then give in and take a permanent nap.

Toward the end of his career, Cézanne ended up leaving blank, unpainted areas, giving the eye a place to roam, to invent our own endings, or take refuge in his not-knowing. He became interested in deliberately unfinished work, in space as "substance." These new landscapes and portraits left whole corners of exposed canvas, only the primer showing through like an air grate with unexpected blasts of musty heat from a speeding train.

Cézanne's previous technique of layering on thick, protruding brushstrokes that were like a fox chasing its tail in the snow, with each paw print leaving deep indents in the ground, slowly receded and revealed what gets left out, what isn't there to be found, what is lacking, and therefore what is endlessly fascinating because it lives in the gaps.

The Hermitage has a Cézanne I especially loved as a child depicting his mother and sister. It's called *Girl at the Piano* and looks like a solemn tea-stained dream of a young woman in a white dress sitting sideways at a piano with the mother doing a bit of sewing on the red divan to the right. I hated to play my violin and would have chosen to learn the piano if we could have afforded one for me to practice on. Because I wished you were the peaceful and settled type of mother who could sit long enough to hear me play for her, this painting was what I practiced telling people you were really like underneath.

No one at school dared to probe me about your absence. Friends or teachers weren't willing to ask for the truth and hear my lies, but I practiced many stories about you for years to come anyway, this still being my favorite narrative—that you're happy just to be in the same room with me and you have nowhere else to go, that I can play stunning music without practicing, that you watch me become a grown-up.

Cézanne died of pneumonia, his lungs sinking in a swampy chest. He insisted on working out in the fields for hours after a heavy downpour had begun and was revived after the initial collapse. He intended to keep tilling the earth after a painting session with a live model but was never able to leave his bed again.

My mother has never seen *Girl at the Piano* with me. This would be the ultimate collapse of the fourth wall.

× × × ×

Once he won the bureaucratic paper war and had sufficiently proven that he wasn't able to get equitable employment and was persecuted for his culture, religion, and skin color in Russia, my father became obsessed with acquiring local art to take along with us overseas. He had a number of painters come to our apartment and spread out unframed canvases along our wall-length shelving in the living room. My father said that most of them were alcoholics and sold their paintings cheap and fast to get more vodka. I decided to tell people that my mother was an artist after that. I took whatever true fragment of that sentence could be useful for my fictional story and ran with it. I added it to my visions of the future "us" captured so eloquently by Cézanne's hand.

In the weeks before our departure for Vienna as the porthole to our permanent home, with our citizenship officially renounced, barely eleven years old, I got sent out to fetch a small painting of a bird coming back to her nest. The egg was a real pearl set into the chunky oils.

I had to travel from our place on Bronnitskaya to Nevsky Prospect, a major thoroughfare on one of the islands in the center of town. I found the right guy at one of the stalls and gave him all the money I had on me. Staring at the protrusions on the canvas, I managed to get myself lost after missing my home subway stop. I stood in a doorway outside a station I didn't recognize, clutching the painting under my arm and contemplating how to get the extra fare I now required, when a teenage girl who tapped the side of her bicep with a folded umbrella approached me with offers of a place to stay; she explained what she did with old men for money and how well I would do if I came away with her—a runt offered a trick tit.

I stared at her umbrella as though it were an exposed lung rhythmically pumping with oxygen. It began to rain, and she invited me in for shelter. Her eyes were static. I ran to the metro and begged a stranger to give me the fare.

My dad was napping on the couch with a bent elbow over his face when I finally arrived with the painting. He was completely spent

from his recent battles to secure us visas. He had thrown out his
back as usual when stressed.

A few months before, Dad had managed to go overseas to visit his
best friend, who got married to a Japanese man she had met in
Russia and was able to send my father a visa immediately after her
citizenship was established. Dad saved up a considerable amount
of money from seeing therapy clients privately in our flat. He had
been robbed and threatened before and felt that he could invest this
money by purchasing a car in Japan and having it shipped to Leningrad. He would learn how to drive on his own somehow.

We brought a couple of friends and a bottle of champagne to the
loading dock to pick up his white Toyota when the pod finally arrived. One of them had driven a Russian Zhiguli and was quite lost
dealing with this car, the steering wheel on the right instead of on
the left. It was a bold move on Dad's part. He could have been killed
by thugs for having a foreign car. Or if he were assumed to be richer
than he was, I could have been taken for ransom.

We all feared the car would be stolen. Instead, Dad wrecked it.
He totaled it in a head-on collision driving to Moscow for his final
American consulate meeting, where they would either offer him
a refugee visa or reject his file without the remaining evidence he
had to bring forth. He walked away from the car crash with minor
bumps and bruises. He had fallen asleep at the wheel, too exhausted
to pay attention, pushing on for what he thought would be the last
of the final pushes.

When Dad talks about our history together, he will say that this is his favorite part of our legend. It's the part where he comes back home to Leningrad on the train. He tells me that everything is ruined, that he failed, and we may not get to leave for America after all. That he wrecked our Toyota and there is no insurance, that we have nothing left, the bargaining chip had been bargained away and we should bear down into the hopelessness. Lacking any ambivalence, I will embrace him at once and announce that "We can always get new things, but I can never get a new dad. I only care that you are alive."

I have seen ten snowy seasons by now. I am about to enter fifth grade. I have an unrequited crush on a timid boy whose mother looks soggy and slurs her words. I have been left home alone for years and continue to get to boarding school and back on my own without question. I don't care about leaving my country. I haven't been held by my mother in months and months. I don't need more things or people to miss. I can no longer imagine who or what is to be missed in a blind alley *toska*. Elena is a north wind madness kicking me around.

I suppose I do long for my mother, but being her copy is like having the flu in the morning, early-onset dementia in the afternoon, and a post–car wreck concussion at night.

XVII

When I am taken from Elena for good she will walk through the dust of what used to be a country of war victory parades, crimson carnation wreaths, state-issued wool underpants, tombs of embalmed Communist party leaders, ration coupons, children dancing around sunlamps, Vanka Vstanka tilting dolls, Olympic bear souvenirs, forbidden denim, and rock music. The dignity in the collective. Kvass and beer keg stations parked on the way to the subway, a drunk and sober line formed in the morning each time the weather warmed up.

The frigid November day my father and I are exiled as political refugees from the Soviet Union he is thirty-two years old. My parents' age difference is almost the length of a typical fetal gestation: forty weeks.

A pinched daughter who leaves her mother in the fall will have a cold German winter awaiting her arrival in Vienna in 1989. Will have a passport that is made only to be taken away at the airport, a refugee status for a refuse with a suitcase of sardine tins and cured sausages, and a new children's Bible stuffed in her hand by the heel-of-the-bread-faced missionaries. Will have a mother who was asked no permission to have her bad seed taken from her cracked shell, now buried and gone in the wet muck leaf heap. But the daughter wasn't stolen goods if the mother didn't notice her absence for some time.

A sensible leaver, Susan Sontag allows her son to be raised by his father, purposefully, unlike my mom, so that she can think clearly and write about art, Russia, class, morality, photography, and death. Sontag only kept photos of people whose work she admired on her desk instead of family portraits. I will do the same for some time to come, arranging a sleuth wall of connections that may seem incongruent to Elena's heritage, but any thread of a woman on the margins is an incantation of motherhood in our case. About exiles like mine, Sontag wrote that "What followed in the wake of 1989 and the suicide of the Soviet empire is the final victory of capitalism."

I will land on the winning side of a distasteful history with aisles of cheerfully arranged products to wander around and play hide-and-seek with your shame. No class, no country, no family pictures to be had. Nothing familiar to eat. New slogans. Eat me.

What does one get as the first meal after your child goes missing? What would I force myself to consume if my children were stolen away from me? What was the first bite of food that touched my mother's lips after she was stripped of her maternal rights? The last supper is an elaborate ritual, a feast leading to the death of a future god. Mine would have to be bar peanuts with a cheap beer. My mother, I imagine, ate deviled eggs or peas.

I barely remember the day we didn't say goodbye, shortly before the jubilant collapse of the Berlin Wall. We were in Granny Galina's small foyer with coats layered on thick by the mirror to the left of the doorway. She kneeled down and cried, trying not to hug too tightly.

Granny looked up at my dad and begged him to wait a few hours, or until tomorrow, to give my mother a chance to turn up for a real farewell. "Until tomorrow," my dad said, picking me up, worth my weight in wet feathers. And so, *Until tomorrow* is what I keep.

These days, I think of *ma*, a Japanese word that doesn't have a precise translation but is roughly the "gap, pause, or space between two structural parts." One can be conscious of a place, not as a hemmed-in, three-dimensional entity, but as form and formlessness coexisting as an interval, between breaths, between destruction and rebuilding, between resting and looking again.

Most Soviet apartments had inner and outer doors and windows as a method of providing both extra insulation and additional refrigeration. We stored our preserves and pickles in between doors or windows. There was a built-in shelf to the right as you came in through the heavy black door. No, there was a shelf to the left as you left. It stealthily held our winter hopes in jars.

The sours. The bitters. The salts. The brines.

XVIII

Gabriel makes many lists.

Like my father, I like lists because long explanations irritate me, and I enjoy crossing things off. Long explanations irritate me because I am still your child, impatient, never actualized as taller than your chest, looking up, hot face, waiting. I enjoy crossing things off because I have never been to your grave and I desire finish lines to help me know how endings can be achieved.

He writes down what we need to bring on our journey out of Russia. We forget those things, or we have to make more room for them, but can't. We shuffle around the sausages in the suitcase yet again in an attempt to fit more preserved foods. We give away red leather-bound books that we had read many times over. What's left of the rare stamp collection after a neighborhood boy my father once took under his wing rips off the priciest series. Uncle Chanukah gets our furniture, arranged and rearranged over the years along the maroon-and-gold wallpaper we hung ourselves. My favorites: the mirrored armoire where I hid away hard candy, and the desk my father sat behind doing paperwork as I sheepishly came in one night to ask him for a bandage, my badly sliced thumb behind my back, after using his shaving razor to carve out some velvet for a doll's dress from a ring box I wasn't to touch.

We keep our paintings, because the art means we are going to do much more than survive the journey ahead. My father has special crates built for them. We will have to check in at customs early, as they are to be shipped to more than one destination. A final destination yet unknown. No finale for our open-ended dyad. Bringing along Suzie—a cocker spaniel we bought shortly before receiving our visas—pointed toward a wishful abundance, an empty peacocking, but a good pose nonetheless. Gabriel didn't have to hide yearning for status and standing any longer. He could Oscar Wilde–out to his fullest, embellish only everything worth desiring for in his impoverished state.

Our photo albums we forget on top of the wardrobe chest because we are too tired and frazzled that morning. If "the problem is not that people remember through photographs, but that they remember only the photograph," as Sontag writes, our failure to bring along the albums would further remove us from our inheritance, our documented events. Our people would be alive in our verbal archive only. This diptych would have to be enough.

I guzzle down some Pepsi and it hits my nose better and harder than the American version ever will. We are ready to go.

We left you behind, but you were never invited.

During our customs inspection out of the Soviet Union Dad hid jewels in my ears behind a strategically styled shag haircut I hated.

"Gypsies keep gold and other valuables in their mouths," he tells me. "Be lip to lip."

He stuffed some foreign bills he had exchanged on the black market into the ski boots I wore, ignorant of their versatility. When he came out of the little examination room where he got strip-searched, he was gray-skinned and wild-eyed. He grabbed my hand and pushed on with purpose. He tucked his shirt back in, drew in some air, and petted Suzie, faking a brisk smile. We were lucky no one noticed the little mule with the currency, a future of conversions, shifting foot to foot.

We were given visas and one-way tickets to Austria, then Italy, and finally America because we were darker than the other Russians in Leningrad. Because he came over from the Caucus region and married a white Christian woman. Because I'm not Jewish according to the Jews, but I'm Jewish according to the Soviet Union. It is written so on the first page of our oxblood canvas passports with bent corners and a hammer and sickle framed by a golden wreath.

My father was once offered a prestigious spot as a psychotherapist soon after graduation. The human resources department needed his passport. They had assumed he was Azerbaijani, which was also part of his ethnicity. When the lady at the front desk came back with his passport and said the position had been filled, he begged her to tell him if it was because of the second thing marked under NATIONAL-ITY. She didn't make eye contact and firmly, yet gently, tried to shoo him away. He didn't know if he was supposed to bribe his way out of being a Jew or if this was an instance where such a move could get him thrown out of the Communist Party, one more mark against a comrade on his official documents.

Our Soviet-Jewish passports would be given up for Alien IDs. Demean. Undermine. Obstruct. Abandon. That was our refugee cycle of airports.

Some exiled Russians have been said to die because of a shattered heart—hyperbole and melodrama are our enamel miniature brooches pinned on chests after the Lenin pins are stripped and sold off to foreigners itching for Soviet kitsch. It's a collective *toska*. A longing for Mother Russia that can become fatal. Take me back or I'll die. Loving one's country, serving one's country, dying for one's country are all an honor and a privilege. These must have been great men, patriots. They watched with disgust as new maps were made after the Soviet regime was ousted, their country shrinking its borders, birthing prisoner countries they claimed as fibroid tumors to bleed out a bigger picture.

Take me back or I'll die isn't a threat that ever works.

On the plane, I watch my dad's eyelids glisten like blintzes draped over blueberries. Sometimes I'm still that child, writing my mother letters with blank envelopes, splitting off into voices heard and imagined, hoping it's all the poetry I recited as a young Russian pioneer with my hand at my forehead saluting the red flag—Always Ready. When the plane lands in Vienna, the place Jews like us tried to escape, I will not ask about my mother.

I will not ask for her until I speak English without an accent and grow breasts and fall in love for the first time and consider using my body for pleasure with another person, and that body will make me think of her, how it was given to me through her lust and labor pain. I will become unmute at last. I will ache at the source. And I'll try to see her. I will give birth twice in lieu of going back again and again to my first home, believing she is there waiting for me, staring at the door with knitting in her lap.

XIX

After a few months on the outskirts of Vienna we arrived in Italy at a refugee camp of little unheated cabins at a summer soccer training ground, later moving to a rented flat with other Russians when no one would sponsor our visa to America. Long after all of our friends were granted asylum in Israel, Western Europe, or the US, we were the last ones left, not so much standing as slumping over in our lull. We were four-day-old fish. My Italian trip gave my growing thighs caked-on nightmares and a new wish to add to the bottle bobbing out in the open seas, never meeting shores, never docking at my mother's port.

We were placed in a town called Lida di Ostia, which, as the name says, is a beauty by the sea, approximately an hour outside of Rome. My dad got a job pumping gas at an Esso station and I was a squeegee-and-mop window girl on busy street corners. He explained that we desperately needed all the money I would make washing windows in order to get a head start in the States. I had just turned twelve, already the secondary breadwinner in our household.

Incredibly dirty men in cars would wave money at me. When I came over to take it, I would see that their trousers were undone, and they held their dicks in their hands. The really old guys were usually dressed in dapper khaki suits or linen button-downs and the dicks they waved like wrinkled flags back and forth were flaccid, all out of girl-harassment juice, but the desire to participate was still there. I would grab the money out of their free hand and run, setting up shop on a different corner.

Rome was a big city, and my eyes were peeled for corners where other kids weren't hustling cars for window washings, or worse still, for sex. I did and didn't know why some of the kids actually got into these men's cars. I always only took the money and ran. Even though I hated washing car windows at red lights and running away with the money when I saw old dicks, my dad promised me ice cream at the end of the day if I made a certain amount of money. I was afraid to buy my own treats and felt guilty about skimming off the top when I did. The gelato in Italy is outstanding, a tangible marker of worth. I went back out on the street each time he fretted about bills and I made us the money. I gave it to him, pleased with any reward, a sign of belonging, of gratitude. I looked forward to the eventual exhale of going home with my dad at dusk. Maybe we would stroll the promenade and pick mussels for supper by the bearded rocks.

I was all alone in a strange country save for my dad and the friends he made. One of the single moms in his refugee circle had a son my age who was also barely parented, allowing us to sneak around the streets of Ostia at night and steal gas caps off as many cars as we could before our flour sacks became too heavy and we stashed them in abandoned boats on the shore. Walking back home we snickered and pointed at all of the parked cars lined up by the boardwalk with the fogged-up windows rocking gently like the sea on the horizon behind us.

The layers of danger we caused seemed laughable in our catcall fish-bowl, either physically pursued by strangers or observing the casual vulgarity postered over our innocence, ignored. We were eventually caught in the act—finally seen and noticed as the unruly mutts with their leashes chewed off—forced to walk around town and restore every cap we could salvage to its proper function. To remember the source of the theft or keep twisting random covers around holes on vandalized cars until the right one found its home was somehow restorative.

In the summer of 1990, on our last full day in Italy, before we were to finally reach the promised land of cold, cold soda pop and hard living, my father's boss invited only me over for dinner at his place.

My father had let me go without hesitation. The boss said he had a travel bag to gift me so I could pack up the knickknacks and hand-me-downs we had acquired on Sundays at the local church, when the Catholic charity fed us lasagna and opened up white rooms with old angora sweaters in neat stacks, no-longer-starched button-down shirts, and knit dresses with tiny moth holes in them delicately arranged across plywood fold-out tables.

Every piece of clothing, which smelled like honeysuckle perfume spilled onto just-used old-ladies' foam hair rollers, my father and I stuffed into paper bags and stored in the mirrored closet of our Ostia flat. We were hoarding these things to possibly resell them later. My father was also saving the clothes as future presents for my stepmother, who had succumbed to a heroin addiction, along with her younger sister. In the meantime, he was going to give out some of the loot to his fillers-in, his minor conquests in between the dry spells.

I was excited to get a new travel bag and I was hungry.

We ate dinner with his twenty-year-old daughter. Afterward she spread out on the floor in front of us, watching television on her stomach with her flat feet facing the ceiling like a perched butterfly. We sat behind her on a beige sofa with the plastic covers on. He draped his arm around my shoulder—no more than the length of an orange—with his enormous palm landing at my chest. He rubbed around the smooth surface and gave me a conciliatory pat on the raisin dot of a nipple and sat up.

He took me into his bedroom. I followed him in without protest. He laid me down on his carefully made-up bed. Everything in the room looked like vanilla pudding, save the simple Jesus on a cross hanging above the headboard. I stared at it like a speedometer that went flat right as the brakes failed. He began licking me and looking up for my reaction. There was something white on his lips. He tried to fit himself inside me but somehow couldn't or wouldn't. The hole in the wall was too tough to prod. He stood me up and tried to figure me out like a keyhole that wouldn't accept the break-in. He could have just ripped off the doorjamb but seemed too proud to make that much of an effort or create a scuffle. It was a seduction with an unfortunate detour in his eyes. A preteen conjecture.

A Pentimento rape.

He was puzzled. He shrugged. He clutched my hand, and we left his bedroom. His daughter was still on the floor. The television sounded like home, like a mother ship, the chirping of the only song I still knew by heart when this new deafness, blindness, muteness came over me.

Not quite deflowered, but plucked and tossed away.

He walked me down to his cellar, not wanting to leave me upstairs with his oblivious daughter. I thought that this would be when he would kill me. He couldn't fuck me, so he would kill me. He didn't turn on the lights. He fished around the dusty, termite-chewed-up shelves for the blue canvas bag he had assured me was still mine when the search went on a tad too long, when I wouldn't take my left hand off the rail by the entrance. He walked me back to the Esso station to meet my dad at the end of his shift, and the three of us posed for a farewell photo. My already emaciated dad was all oblivious skin on bone that day, still without dinner, light enough for liftoff.

x x x x

When my great-granny Hope died I watched her in the coffin and imagined myself, or my mother, in it one day. A mother who won't come home and is sleeping on a park bench drinking cologne in the snow is a dead mother walking.

I knew how to lie down, how to stand up, but I never kneeled then.

Mother, I am now down on my knees, Audre Lorde asking for me, *To whom do I owe the woman I have become?* when being taken from you is what marks the end of girlhood.

In the photo of us sitting on the floor at the airport in Rome, I am wearing a yellow sweat suit and straddling a baby-pink and sky-blue stuffy of a dog, while Dad is holding on to my light-gray stuffed animal with pleading puppy cartoon eyes and floppy ears. Dad is powering the grid of his dazzling teeth with a teenage boy's smile. My bag is visible next to us in the center of it all. My other Italian toys poke out of the opened zipper.

I woke up a few times on the plane headed for Philadelphia. You

could still smoke on planes then and the dirty gauze of spent Dunhills scratched my eyes open. I couldn't stop staring at the bag that
man gave me as my dad unpacked it later at the motel on our first
day of my new air-conditioned America. With me, inside, was the
country of the blockade, of Stalin, of unmarked graves, mass graves,
scattered ashes, the Tomb of the Unknown Soldier, pressed flowers,
ghost cipher mothers who needed to hear my secrets.

I think I woke up in Spanish class years later when we were learning the word *molestar* and I realized the teacher had been calling
on me over and over. She wanted to know where I had gone. I had
been in that cellar to be sure. In the cellar again, with that blue
bag, which is still at my father's house. I think I woke up in the
middle of reading my Cookie Mueller book in which she said that
her rapist sucked at the crime but gave her a musical jewelry box
with a twirling pink ballerina inside before she escaped onto the
streets of San Francisco. "It wasn't even done well," she remem-
bers. Alerting the hippies she ran to on Haight about her distress,
they fed the guy a massive dose of acid and claimed his gun as
vengeance. No such luck for me, a souvenir forged without a rescue squad.

Nearly being killed, nearly being raped, is like constantly smelling
the rotting food you can't find in your fridge every time you open the
door to get something new to eat. Your appetites have been trashed.

The women in my family always planned to eat onions on the nights
they wouldn't be kissing men. The odor too repellant, unfeminine.

But some nights, Granny and Mom would just shrug it off, cutting up whole bulbs for their herring, cry-laughing and rinsing knives under cold water to lessen the sting.

Traveling alone as a woman can still get you raped and killed. Traveling a few yards to a nearby field, even with a friend, or sister, or cousin in tow just so you can take a shit can get you raped and hanged. Skinned to drip-dry like a rabbit.

Hordes of writers dream of going to Italy in order to find themselves, find their new voice. And because, up until very recently, women couldn't travel alone at all, this may be a worthy pursuit if you can afford it. Supervised travel used to be done in order to become cultured and more interesting to your future husband (sadly, matrimony is where most of the protagonists of modern travel writing eventually end up anyway) and had to be done quickly before your body shriveled up. Before you were to give birth to more kids than you wanted, or knew to want, and die somewhere between one of your children's first days and weddings.

Dorothy Richardson, my patron saint of women on the hunt for adventure—an elliptical purpose constructed by going above the nerve—arrived in New York City alone to live in shabby little rooms and moved around constantly to afford her next meal. She had to be quite a bit terrified. Writing hunger and loneliness. Recording every meal with waning ink and patience, her wet hem never really drying from obsessively searching the streets for work, then stoking a small fire and making a record of that hem for me before slipping into cold sheets for the night.

James Joyce's *Ulysses*, written in a stream-of-consciousness technique he supposedly perfected, would overshadow Dorothy Richardson, who already walked as she talked as she wrote, making sentences open like blasting for river dams long before him.

Odysseus's name means *trouble* in Greek, after the disastrous giving and receiving of misfortune throughout his wanderings. The word *odyssey* refers to an epic voyage in many languages. But what do you call a voyage with a constant fear of rape, of your story getting submerged? Every pit stop a landmine?

Inland bravery before shipwrecks.

I do not like travel writing, the doing or the reading. My own eye-rolls around women's precarious safety and nauseating domesticity spat and cursed at within a lucid dream-state that is like the seasickness of trauma, my own cold case investigation—a childhood as the evidence locker—didn't help my courage one bit.

Renata Adler's work was compared to a strange type of travel writing, with little quips of observation in a touch-and-go manner of sketching a scene here, a restaurant there, impressions of people elsewhere. Instability. Velocity. Refuge. Disjointedness. The only kind of narrative in motion I can stomach—defamiliarized.

I cannot synthesize place and words, the two things I enjoy and struggle with most. Like bad plasma attacking the immune system. Let me describe Leningrad or Portland to you in detail and watch me vanish through expansion.

The fourth state of matter. A sense of place. Paradise. Hell. I choose a pregnant purgatory.

XX

A year after I last saw you I was ushered into some tavern attached to a cheap motel for my first breakfast in a new country where a beautiful bald woman sang on a television mounted in a dark corner like she was talking to only me. She had such well-formed, singular tears pulsing out of her eyes. There were jugs of Pepsi, clinking with ice cubes, and two kinds of cold cereal to choose between.

The people in this air-conditioned strange land seemed to be loose in the joints, seemed to be casual, seemed warm without any heat, seemed to be cool, cool enough to know that Sinéad O'Connor was in fact covering a Prince song, the name of which said two things at once: I compare nothingness to you, and I can only judge the square in relation to the round hole inside of it. *"Nothing Compares 2 U."*

The lady in the black square box reminded me of you. I didn't know what she was saying at the time, but it gave me swells and curdles in the belly. I wondered where you were, and I was also used to not wondering, so the feeling was of swimming through mud, of floating in something slimy, but floating nonetheless.

No one had asked me or knew that my underwear was part of an old bathing suit and hadn't been changed in a week. That I smelled like souring, like expired food. I wanted the lady on the television to change my underwear. I wanted to know what clean felt like here in America without you.

I was told by my dad to lie and continue saying I was Jewish even after I found out in seventh grade, at the first school I attended in America, the Hebrew Academy, that goyim are the ones like me.

As I got better at reading and writing in Hebrew I learned that numbers tell a complicated tale of *our* legacy and there is a secret code that only a few men can formally study. We have our four mothers to look up to: Sarah, Rebekah, Leah, and Rachel. Four children ask four questions while four cups of wine are drunk at Passover.

My own obsession with numbers was seeded at the Hebrew Academy when my dad insisted I drill the multiplication table with him. I kept fumbling, too slow with the answers. Dad sat down on the couch and put me on a stool in front of him. He explained that this is going to be a new game. I have a certain amount of time to come up with the right answer or he will knock me off the stool. My answers didn't come soon enough. Four by four is sixteen. Five by five is twenty-five. Six by six is on the floor.

In junior high I understood enough English to discern that your Jewishness is carried through your mother's bloodline. That a Jewish man like my father can go around impregnating all the Christian girls he wants and still not be properly fruitful or multiplying. That the penalty for goyim who secretly study the Torah is to be a slave building the wall of the messiah's palace in their afterlife; that my father picked the wrong woman and now it was up to me to light candles as a fake, a good reproduction of a well-known painting snuck into a museum with the originals.

I liked to lie about you because I was used to closely watching the other boys and girls around me to see what felt right to imitate, what I could get away with. We are supposed to emulate our parents until they make it safe for us to reject them. Then we carve out our own shape from the boulders we once found at the feet of their mountains.

A lie is its own language, a skin graft. Roland Barthes proposed that "language is a skin: I rub my language against the other. It is as if I had words instead of fingers, or fingers at the tip of my words. My language trembles with desire." My deepest desire then is to cover you up where you are naked, to give you skin where you are invisibilized, because no one else dares to rub two words together to make you appear. Not least of all, my stepmother.

× × × ×

Luda was only twenty-five when my father reconciled with her. They had parted ways on the understanding that her chances of emigrating as a Ukrainian woman with no documentation of persecution, in-demand skills, or resources, save her connection to us, noncitizens, were scant at best. With the yoke of Communism all but ripped off, our old country was now in freefall. She flew in from Russia on a visitor's visa to Philadelphia, shortly before we all moved to Brooklyn, and stayed on for good. Luda watched *Sleeping with the Enemy* and wrote out the details of their arguments in her diary, looking up from time to time to reassure me that we get to split things fifty-fifty, now that she had come back to lighten my burden. As long as I tell her everything, mainly any dirt I have on my dad. The secrets would spill out of her the minute he was back from washing dishes at the sports bar in between his TOEFL classes, our table flying in the air as he denied ever bedding those other women, mayonnaise jar going splat on the wall, dripping down, his head in hands as the brown carpet absorbed the grease.

She was my anchor, my rival, and a sister-mother-friend hybrid of sorts. She is only twelve years older than me, so whenever we used to lie about her being my real mom, the reactions—and our varying explanations—ranged from awkward to hilarious to downright sad. The new friends we made in America wished to know the secret of her unlined face, how she managed to look so fresh while having a teenage daughter. If she thought that becoming close with a person was a possibility, Luda would press my face into her stomach and whisper to the person about our situation of motherhood musical chairs, asking them to keep up our charade.

Luda was finally granted the chance to have a biological child of her own the summer between my junior and senior years at John Dewey High School. She was tired of grazing like a parasitic bee and wished to be "like any other normal woman." I was instantly smitten with this pink rubbery scream machine and took on the role of a secondary mother when Luda struggled with a violent bout of postpartum depression, staring out into the darkness on the couch, eyes shining with terror like a shivering snare drum as the baby wailed on. I instinctively stuck him in a pram, which I pushed around our Bensonhurst blocks for hours before heading off to class.

Many years later, after Luda had given birth to a daughter as well and my half brother learned to count, he added things up. He asked me how old I was. He knew how old she was. He did the finger math in front of me as we drove around the Connecticut countryside. The number he arrived at was twelve—extended pause. He didn't believe that *our* mother could have given birth to me as a child, much like any girl in his class.

When I was twelve, I had just begun to get some perky little boobs while Luda was still decidedly flat chested. I once gave her rolled-up socks and told her to stick them in her bra so that we could match. It was an especially low blow since she didn't even wear one. She threw them across the breakfast table and screamed that men can get by without boobs just fine. Knowing she meant *Your dad gets along without boobs just fine*, I put the socks in my own bra and strutted around the apartment making kissy faces at her.

Luda would primp in the mirror, standing on her bed with arms bent behind her head, tasting the fabric of new American cuts with her skin. I watched her from the doorway while drinking milk. "I wish there was a pill we could take that would make us feel full and pumped with nutrients so that our grocery budget can be spent on dresses and shoes," she purred. "Milk has cholesterol in it. Actual pieces of fat floating around. Just know that when you lap it up every day."

This was the beginning of our acrimonious sisterhood when I needed a mother figure most. Taking turns acting cruel and needy, we called each other whores one moment, then undesirable the next—eternal girls being looked at, but not really seen. Back when noticing my suddenly plumper thighs as I sat up in bed to put my slippers on shocked me into pinching them to make sure they were really mine. When she gave me a blue satin thong, hoping to inspire more glamour into my overall wardrobe, I found its implications so tyrannical and its shape so utterly useless that I hid it inside of an old boot.

And when I got my period at a birthday party minutes after a boy gave me a kiss on the cheek, I ran home to Luda pulsing on adrenaline, pimple scars covered by greasy bangs, thick and black. We traded some food stamps for cash and got the thinnest pads at the dollar store and had enough left over for two containers of Chinese food to share in bed.

Luda was jubilant and pragmatic, helping me get cleaned up and cuddling me in her bed after. And then came her usual words of wisdom: "Well, I guess you are now officially a woman." Squinting at the sun reflected off her vanity mirror, I smiled and mushed my face into her neck. "And you must be careful, because above all, this means that your body is ready for pregnancy." I scrunched my toes to numb and gritted my teeth hard.

Shortly after I got my period Luda and I walked across town, pushing on and dripping through the haze of a scorching summer day to get her an abortion. My father kept stalling her back then: he wasn't ready, he already had a child, we were broke, and their fights were out of control.

On the way to the abortion clinic, one of us bled. Two on the way back.

XXI

Bernadette Mayer put out her *The Desires of Mothers to Please Others in Letters* in 1994 while you begged for my address to write me, maybe please me. My uncle will claim that he was under strict orders to not give out our *danuye*—my exact whereabouts were to remain a secret, but she was allowed to look at the most recent photos of me.

It was in my father's desk drawer, right before I left for college, that I found some pictures of you, including the passport photo he furtively kept there, the kind printed as a set of four.

I have another photo of you stashed in a book, hidden in a closet, buried behind some boxes. You are perched on a kitchen sink in a dark room with people dancing in the background, staring straight into the camera with your head cocked back. You're smoking and reaching out toward the photographer, oblivious to being approached for a hug. In the corner of the frame we see the back of your little daughter wearing a tight terry-cloth jumper and running for your feet.

I began using a computer for the first time as a senior to manage the layout for a feminist quarterly Dewey miraculously supported and printed since its inception in the 1970s. I never had thought about email or going online. In fact, I arrive at The Evergreen State College having seen photos of the place only in a catalog.

Before I leave our apartment in Brooklyn I ship my favorite records and books ahead to my dorm in Olympia and pack my clothes.

America in the 1990s is: thigh highs. Orange velvet trench coat with wide lapels. Lee cutoffs from the five-dollar bin at Canal Jeans with ripped tights. Ringer T-shirt with the word BITCH written in myriad fonts. Navy-blue polka-dot baby doll dress. White turtleneck bodysuit. Nude-colored satin nightgown with bell sleeves from the 1930s. Army surplus olive-green backpack with patches. Doc Martin knee-high lace-up boots. White communion dress with cutoff sleeves and ripped hem. Plastic flowers tied to suede platform shoes. Brown acrylic men's cardigan with holes in the cuffs. Fishnet stockings with crotch cut out, worn with legs for sleeves. Lilac-colored T-shirt with BIKINI KILL written in bleach.

Black slip worn over white lace-trimmed slip. Red crepe ball gown cut above the knee. Boatneck striped long-sleeve shirt over ballet tights. Baby-blue sparkle halter dress soaked with sweat from the Limelight.

I get a work-study job at Evergreen as an office assistant to a woman in charge of campus security. She tells me to check her email daily and give her a digest of the most pertinent correspondences. I am too ashamed to tell her that I have never used email. I take naps on stacks of manila envelopes and wait for her to fire me, which she does, within a week.

I scan the back pages of the local weekly paper and circle an ad for a peep show. I am eighteen years old and have been speaking English without a Russian accent for four years. I worked hard to lose it by studying TV shows, *The Bionic Woman*, a favorite, and recording movies like *Beetlejuice* with a lo-fi cassette player, copying ironic, maudlin teenage sayings to fit in, and unironically wearing a Purple Haze *Simpsons* T-shirt with an American flag–printed blue jean miniskirt handed down by the family who sponsored our visa. In high school gym class, I told a girl to "not have a cow, man" when she face-planted trying to jump the horse.

She was red for me, and her redness lets me know I should be ashamed.

I had lived in America for only six years at the time of my arrival in Olympia. No one would ever suspect I was a foreigner, that I was infiltrating their scene with my Russian spy secrets covered up by an already changing Brooklyn accent, and that I was into reproduction art as a means of supporting my tenuous place on earth.

My friend B sold some of her paintings so she could afford to get her giant boobs cut off. As a butch woman in the nineties she was a most glorious "fake," like the "fakes" who bought new boobs—all of us just sucking off each other's discarded selves and making new ones—statue composites that have scars, stitches, and jagged outlines, and reveal the act of simulation, making us paranoid at being found out when someone doesn't fall under our fictive spell. Interlopers as vulnerability experts.

She understood that forgery is the most authentic way to sign off.

During a visit home from college with a new friend brought along as my security blanket against the parents I seldom phoned or wrote, I began displaying new signs of missing you. On the staircase of my family's old basement apartment in Brooklyn I showed my friend your picture and told her that this was my real mother. Years went by with my stepmother being icy to me before she confessed overhearing my conversation and feeling frozen out of my life. The silent agreement we had made to tell people that she was my only mom, that there was no one else, was fractured.

Luda had sacrificed her vanity during the ripest days of her youth, pretending to be older to make the lie of my legitimacy more believable. I collapsed the fourth wall of this act without her permission and she felt exposed and cast aside for a found relic excavated among her husband's desk drawers.

× × × ×

In his posthumously assembled *Mourning Diary*, Roland Barthes attempted to privately express his grief over the death of a mother he knew so well that describing her was an act of violence he could not perform. He recorded ordinary quips about missing her on note cards, sometimes trailing off midsentence. Barthes left the saturation of visual detail to live on in the many photographs he kept on his desk and wrote about in *Camera Lucida*, in which he eulogized her properly to the public. He had searched through stacks of images of her long enough to uncover "the one" where she appeared most alive to him.

Sometimes I use note cards, completely uncataloged and strewn about in ten different purses, on two desks, inside books, old files, and nightstands. They are orphan drafts that I gather up and try to straighten out every now and then, tell them they will grow up in my competent hands and become useful someday; that they will be known and understood, maybe even loved and cared for, spoken about, and not for. But I fail. I fail at this all the time. They get lost. For the most part, no one gets to know them. I lie to the note cards and to myself. *An orphan has no past; a widow has no future.*

I often think of Barthes, who used the card catalog for his writing practice—this handsome gay man avoiding parties at his desk, slowed by his mother's death, getting up and deliberately placing each card where it belongs. That is so fascinating. Such purpose, such ego, such care. I believe that must be something his mother gave him: this importance, this belief, this organization of self and objects. His words are measured, unmoored by grief, but grounded in a place that tells me he was held and loved, that he was once properly managed, assembled by his mother into the person who worships her, who is unable to reduce her to a memory.

I have disparate parts of my writing hidden, lost to be found in old bags and notebooks because it mirrors my own process of mourning my mother, not in her death, of which I have no knowledge, but in what she did and did not provide me in life. Each fragment, bandage-like, papier-mâché, peeling on and off to smear balm and apply fresh swaths of gauze, dressing you like a mummy. The words that used to punch ribbon on a typewriter when I wrote you letters in high school now click away impotently but make pleasing little stacks on the screen.

He collects his thoughts on cards the way he was raised. I collect mine the way I was—the excavation process of the preverbal made solid. "Neither album, nor family," Barthes proclaimed about the act of looking and collecting. He became obsessed with a photo of his mother as a young girl and decided that it was the only image worthy of memorialization. This old woman lives on best as someone's daughter.

XXII

When I lived in Seattle in my early twenties, traveling back to Olympia on the Greyhound bus to finish up college, I worked at a peep show for about four years. It was the only time in my life I drank almost every day. That was the place where I thought, yes, I could die from these hangovers and find her not looking for me at last.

The movie *Frances* came out in 1982, when I was four years old and spending my mornings watching my wet-with-hangover-dew mother and her two dearest accomplices chug vodka out of little juice glasses on a rickety four-legged table.

Frances Farmer's middle name is Elena—my mother's name. My obsession with that movie and the woman it's about managed to elbow and embroider itself into the fabric of my daughter-legacy for good.

Born in Seattle, Frances Elena Farmer was a rebel from a young age. In the 1930s, she penned an essay called "God Dies" and then traveled to the Moscow Art Theater in the USSR on scholarship during a Red Scare. Frances Farmer became a stage and Hollywood actress who was infamous for her heavy drinking. Frances was hospitalized by her mother against her will and insisted that she was raped and abused while committed. Frances is more famous for the rumors she generated than for the art she made.

A guy in my small Seattle music and art community, who is now in a real famous band, made stickers to mock me and put them up all over our neighborhood. He was teaching me a lesson about who gets to speak in public and what last words, last rites, look like. The stickers were of my heavily made-up face torn out from a copy of *The Stranger*. He typed out and pasted the words: *Read my poetry! Understand my feelings!* around the photo of my barely-past-adolescence-pudgy, fakely seductive visage. I was a hoary child in sexy young-woman drag. A few nights before this smear campaign I was drunk at our regular bar with friends and grafittied the bathroom wall, asking the question of whether the guys in the scene treated women like whores and groupies. It seemed like I was merely pointing out the obvious, and it also made my friends laugh. He felt that I was being hostile and implicating nice-enough guys like him in manipulating and using women, that I was harshing his mellow, that there was no reason to put in ink that Seattle barely had any girls playing music in our clubs.

The picture he used came from an advertisement for the place where I worked. They never paid me for using my image in their ads. The first time it happened I was ashamed and indignant and the second time I felt I deserved no better or should just be grateful for the attention. I continued working there for a couple of years after the guy in the band left town, saying that everyone was real jealous of his success. I didn't write any poetry for about a decade.

× × × ×

As my time at the peep show job that consistently ripped me off was coming to an end, I made friends with the girl no one liked. My other girlfriends wouldn't even order takeout with her. Her father was a minister who broke down her bedroom door and fisted the devil right out of her. Once, on Halloween, she got us both in trouble at work yelling back at the manager after we had arrived late, again, and he charged us an extra stage fee. I planned on hanging out in the dressing room and reading *I Love Dick* instead of hustling shows to avoid the riffraff but found myself back inside her car cooking up ways to replace the money of the lost shift. She wanted to give hand jobs. I wanted to go back home to Olympia.

She became lost driving around talking about our scheme and we ended up in Bellevue. The bridge still gives me the stomach sicks. I dug for sludge in my boots. When we stopped, this girl wanted me to take over and drive back. I didn't have a license. I hadn't yet met my husband, who would eventually teach me how to drive, and I was embarrassed to have skipped this step of proper adulthood. I tried to ward off intrusive thoughts, to believe we couldn't die on the bridge back out to Seattle, but could only picture us flying off into the waves below if I got behind the wheel. We headed for Olympia defeated and stopped over at the sandwich shop where she had a straight job, to pick up her meager paycheck from the few shifts they gave her. She got into a fight with a junkie coworker who played in a local band everyone loved. She was so distracted when she started up the car again that we were hit from my side at the intersection just after going one block.

The firefighters wanted to show me that I had cracked the wind-shield with my head on the passenger side. One of them even said, "See this birdie you put there in the glass?" I hadn't worn a seat belt. I couldn't go to the hospital because I had no insurance, and I was going to be Joan Crawford at a Halloween party at my house. I tried to stay awake doing speed with my favorite queens and faeries for two days to deal with my concussion.

With photography we wish to manage decomposition, seeking out the beloved to force under glass. All of your pictures, too few, are the alien mother-body subjected to material corruption of postbirth ruins. You have been gone, but I didn't know it. Patrick Dubost remarks, "Having found some daguerreotypes on the floor of an attic—portraits eroded by time and light—I know that forgetting is something enormous, that forgetting is our highest destiny." But the body dances out the erosion of the mind.

Girls at the peep show are moiré patterns dancing in a glass box. Pussy refracted refracted refracted to infinity. Indistinguishable intimacy. Shape-shifters. A cliché. Faking it as the balm on the burn.

Clichés have a feeling like snakeskin. Slithery slopes of shedding stale old fat, rising to the surface. The more the snake sheds its skin, the more she hopes the wet and new skin underneath will be the truth; it's the same truth as before, it dries out and fades, but maybe she absorbs the miracle cream of novelty better each time. I could take my clothes off, and the glass box at the peep show gave me new skin.

I already knew the difference between staying and leaving the body, and being only of the mind, and packing that mind in a blue travel bag, and now, a shiny pleather hat box filled with ruffled things, and glittery things, and girly things to take off for money, so I only needed them for a minute but got ready for that minute for an hour.

Jimi Hendrix is asking "Are You Experienced?" over the speakers at the strip place, and I'm nodding Yes. Yes. Yes.

I wanted to be as far away from society as possible, for as long as possible, which meant being self-employed, and there were very few options for me as a teenager when I first began looking for work in college, no parental help or social standing to avoid the trap of long hours with low pay. I didn't want to fake glamour, didn't want to be touched, didn't want to play the games of a typical strip club. The peep show, preferably the cut-and-dried transactional weekday shifts, placed me with women who were just my kind. Counterfeit strippers, caustic with mocking sarcasm, not having any of IT.

In the same spot I used to hide your photo I then carried around a Polaroid of me, Marie, Chantelle, and Brooke, my friends in Seattle, 1998.

My friend Marie is a missing-plane story, like my mom. She took this Polaroid and then we got Indian takeout after. The one out of the frame should get to stay in the picture, the memory of their half-blocked faces as they looked at you in a flash.

What you can see in this family photo are three girls dressed up like strippers. I think we were all bad at real stripping, didn't want to be those girls who were good at it with the pole tricks and tipping the DJ at the end of the night for playing that Guns N' Roses tune and flashing you with warm pink light rather than the green or blue they might throw onto the odd and broke new girls. You can gain the courage to be desperate here.

We used to go to Linda's Tavern on the hill to play dominoes and drink the coldest and largest glass of making you funnier. The four of us girls still girls but angry like gray-dog women. *I want you I want you so bad, come back to me baby, you were my every-thing*, the song, any torch song, my song to block out the jizz-jazz, high-energy pole rockers, goes. Aren't they all kind of the same in their earnestness? We were fearless before we knew the old mat-tresses we slept on were vile with pleasure. We didn't care about gross thrift store–stained cloth touching our bare backs with rakes of mystery, sandpaper-scratched itch. None of us had new dreams and that was the point. The right to remain ambiguous is to split off and perform a new woman, as if in a photo, maybe each time. I cannot perform any mother but the one I made to stand against you.

Four centuries passed before Greek scholars began organizing Sappho's verses into books. Our "largest figure with the smallest remains," quoted and summarized by mouth after mouth, scraps to mirror those of us who are tiny, neglected, truncated trees.

I lived with this picture of my friends, girls like us, Mom, because I didn't have many childhood photos and fear losing any more family portraits. My uncle Chanukah sent us heaps of photos from Russia in the mail when I was a teenager. We received a clear plastic bag with ripped-open manila envelopes that had our address written on them in his neat handwriting. There were three or four water-damaged photos stuck in the corner of the package. The refugees on rafts.

× × × ×

My granny Chaya believed that if we brought our family album along on this journey that a wicked person—an Unclean Force—would lay filthy hands on the visages of our ancestors and living relatives and curse us all. The photos were argued over for hours on the day of our departure.

Neither album, nor family. Photos displayed as taxidermy. The unexplained announced in attempts at gathering.

When Chaya was dying of heart and kidney failure on the same pee-stained couch where I once slept, she asked for me to come and rest my hand on her face and close her eyes.

Her last wish was to see her only granddaughter's face one last time, and so she held on to a picture of me folded into her bosom as she passed.

There are no pictures for these words.

Seattle in 2000 was the place where my leg found a hole in an old, crumbling staircase no one was supposed to use in the back of my house. My bear trap held me captive in consideration of things to come as the flesh swelled against the old wood. I had hives on my neck, a bruise or two each week from diving off barstools, some contact lenses lost behind the eye, two whiskey doubles and ginger back at last call, Dick's burger wrappers strewn about the bed as I got up to check licenses pulled out of wallets to read the names of the mystery guests using my shower. I was twenty-four and in need of a stern warning only my father could deliver. He admired my independence and loathed my aimlessness and secrecy. I was becoming my mother, and he could convince me that ruining myself would not bring her back if I allowed him. He never said this, never mentioned her. I was ready to forgive him, so I applied to the art therapy program at the School of Visual Arts—a compromise between his past career and my present state as an itinerant artist.

I wanted to be cleaned out. I was baptized anew with a flight back to New York City to begin grad school and become an art therapist. The women I worked with at the domestic violence shelter as part of my training never knew that I hid a battered old bird inside a black-breasted sparrow.

I was shy with my new clients, some older, some younger than me, all mothers, and used clay or watercolors or pipe cleaners to get them to talk about their abuse without flooding. The more we worked together the more I saw my Elena in them. I rocked their babies and I encouraged their kids to come to our sessions so that I could fawn over them, sort of hold them at a comfortable distance so that their mothers could see them anew. I watched their touch get softer.

We giggled and hugged when they caught themselves losing their temper over silly accidents. They were lonely, horny, scared, annoyed, and their kids needed to know what lay ahead; they needed the past reinterpreted for them so that it fit, sequentially, contained, back into their heads, heads they banged on the walls, wailing, acting out, begging for a story with a beginning, middle, and end. For a mother who looked for them when they ran away.

XXIII

My father begged me to not go back to Russia. My stepmother threatened to stop speaking to me when she heard I was collecting addresses of friends and family to stay with while searching for Elena. She was curled up with the remote by her side, watching RTN in bed when I came over to get her unattainable blessing, eyes filled with *if you must.* My therapist discouraged me with a reminder that some things are unresolvable, that we fold in on ourselves and regress even when going home for the holidays, even when a frame of reference is stable, your old room and your family stationary, unlike the quicksand of an ill, roving mother in a country that spat me out, bitterly gave me up for a closed adoption to its cooler-than-thou rival.

The idea to go find my mother coincided with finally receiving my American citizenship. My father had gone through the process when I left for college, but I shrugged off the responsibility even as he dutifully mailed me the naturalization applications. There would now be a death of my Alien ID, which had long rendered me unable to leave the country without enormous hassle, and a birth of a passport, removing a substantial obstacle to my journey back. After being sworn in with my future travel companion, whom I had been dating for mere months, as an enthusiastic witness clapping along with the other loved ones in the back rows, I was given all the tools to apply for a passport. I could now hand-grenade my body toward the place where my last passport was confiscated.

I began packing even before I had the tickets—playing pretend. I didn't want to fly back, either, but I wished to be brave, to be done with stillborn fantasies of our delicious reunion. I had a break from school a few months shy of my twenty-sixth birthday, some loan money, and a boyfriend who offered to come along. I didn't choose as much as succumb to the road ahead of me. It was not a hero's journey. I wanted to get it out of the way as fast as possible.

A previous velleity as resignation syndrome.

We all have a propensity for false pattern recognition, to look for meaning, a belief system when mystery is too anxious of a box to contain us—a story that can signify a completeness we have only felt in the darkness of our mother.

"We are dead stars looking back up at the sky," confirms the astronomer Dr. Michelle Thaller.

But she's also reminding me that we are 4 percent of what's left after the last mass extinction, and that your children might face the threat of the next one, while living on the cusp of the golden middle before a blackout.

We can only observe about four thousand stars in our night sky, but stardust collected in a jar will never make us a new planet. It is the loose bits of heat and gravity that create universes out there in the celestial wilderness, the feral, weightless darkness. But our survival depends on reading patterns, on following maps and having a guide, a compass, a cataloged history that we believe will help us predict disasters.

I brought my mother what she may have stolen from me if given half the chance. To be her apparition of a daughter I must be the daughter of fortitude and remember those carefully plucked eyebrows, thin as satin thread. Or her vampy brown lipstick, heavily applied to the doughy, expressive mouth. Or the way she was able to expertly rim her eyes with kohl inside the bottom lash line, making the white of her eyeballs really pop. Or her short bob with silky, chestnut, swoopy bangs combed behind the ear. Or her favorite tight, dark-blue jeans—so hard to scam—that gave her backside a tight pear shape.

Or my dad flirting with her as she walked by the breakfast table in the morning where he was grooming himself with an electric shaver and gave her a quick little buzz on the behind. How she laughed and sort of skipped on one heeled foot as she trotted out of the room. His and Hers Perestroika.

Gabriel and Elena got married in a fever during a late January snowstorm. It was two days after her twentieth birthday. She wore a plain long-sleeved white dress to the courthouse. I was born nine months later. My hernia was protruding so far out that they announced me to my sweaty mother as a boy. "I thought it was your scrotum sack for a second." She enjoyed telling me this story years later along with her other genitalia-related observations. Dad compares their romance to Romeo and Juliet even though they met in a seedy Leningrad bar and it was the bride who took the poisoned drink.

When I packed to come look for her in the fourth year of the second millennium, I thought of that day, and carefully chose enough black lace underwear to last a week, along with some skirts and bras, guessing her size, ready to give her more of what she once wanted— adorning her as a woman needing to push this up and slim that down, of performing a useless restoration of an ill, or possibly dead, mother. As though I would know what condition she was actually in, what state I should be trying to sculpt her back into, using the shards of those brief memories we had together before I left Leningrad as a kid.

After I get done packing I interview my uncle on the phone, who is hazy on dates and details, and get the feeling as though we are gossiping schoolgirls passing silly notes in invisible ink. I scribble down a few disjointed words in what glides out of me as an ancient dialect.

This exchange with Chanukah reminds me of a ubiquitous revolutionary propaganda poster of a stern lady in a kerchief with a finger over her mouth: *Neh Boltay.* Don't Gossip. Rumors can lead to gulags, families liquidated in a matter of days. Antigovernment thoughts or jokes told to a neighbor in confidence can land you in a labor camp. For writers, a poem that might criticize the Russian way of life could get you banned from the union, unable to appear in print again. Your books can be purged and outlawed, or simply phased out as no longer in vogue, like Akhmatova's. There are reasons Russians memorized and recited poetry. Because we wished to express ourselves in a collective stanza as one people against tyranny, a shorthand, and because it could all disappear any minute, so you might as well etch it into your brain and whisper the lyric to your kids in case they never see the pages for themselves.

As a last-ditch effort scouring for more scraps of information I go on an ancestry website and post a desperate message about my upcoming sleuthing trip. Almost immediately, a response from a Russian genealogist pops up:

Found a record which could be of interest to you—

Shalmieva Elena Viktorovna
born 26 Jan 1958
St Petersburg, Bronnitskaya St, house 22, apt 11
Phone +7 812 3161702

The data might be several years old, but still worth a try.

It was a comfort to see our old address attached to her name, from which she was unceremoniously kicked out for pouring vodka on the hearth rather than tending its flames, in every way. The data was indeed too old to be useful, a fading photo with not enough fixer after development.

× × × ×

It is rumored that Sappho had only one child, a daughter who was also dark like her. Somewhere among us there may be Sappho descendants but they have to invent her face, her clothes, her hair, and the lines of her body based on composites of the dress fashion of the times or how she was described centuries later by male poets and scholars who admired her but never met her.

The recently discovered papyrus of Sappho fragments have finally given us more to analyze, assemble, and catalog, but we will always want more fossils. The incomplete has a lifelong contract with our attention span, reminding us of our penchant for endings that create a resolution, our need for excavation of beginnings, our insistence on linearity, our demand for clues of orderliness.

Sappho's poems were once shredded and used as stuffing in mummified royal crocodile carcasses. When found, every bit was pored over with magnifying glasses. Scholars, classicists, archivists, and translators standing around photographs of the ruined text piecing together the elusive message of the woman described as a dark little sparrow. No genuine picture or painting exists of the corporeal Sappho.

The Christians burned her books, proclaiming her a slut. Everything we know about Sappho's familial history or sex life is feminist academic gossip.

Say the word *lyre* out loud.

Anne Carson chose to translate the gaps in her version of Sappho by using brackets. There was a clawlike space to point to the loss, to excite the reader into the potent and excruciating task of wagering bets, of hallucinating a breathing image within a ripped hole.

Bitter words of a love that cannot be mirrored back, a remote love, a dangerously potent love, direct and unwavering in the blank, erased stanzas. A lone line has to signify so much more than its original intention, of a larger lyric, the twenty letters left behind infused and made orgasmic with a meaning that can never be understood.

There can be no periods at the end of Sappho translations because she is forever unfinished business to us

XXIV

I would book the trip during the famous white nights in June, when the bridges part over the canals and it is dusk at four in the morning, the city actually not being able to sleep so people become possessed; they make out on every corner and leave their spouses for anyone who winks at them. I wanted my three-note, sleepy, leveled and depressed but loyal boyfriend to wake up in Russia and never pass out on me again.

The landscape ahead of us: Russia is a blacked-out mother, lifted robe. Three channels in black and white, two of them playing the same thing when the news broadcast is on, a knob that keeps coming off. A motherland unlost, but not found.

Before the glory of the white nights never materialized, because I was mostly paralyzed with dread and feelings of incompetence for not knowing how to find my mother, we managed to board a flight to Moscow, with a connecting flight to St. Petersburg. What I didn't remember from my childhood is that the international and local airports are two separate entities.

There was so much confusion over getting a car to take us to a different part of Moscow that we missed our connecting flight and were forced to sleep on separate beds, watching late-night Russian TV in a crappy motel after a dinner of chicken Kiev so greasy it squirted us in the eye when pressed into with a fork. I couldn't figure out how to get a new chip for my flip phone and let the family friends who went to pick us up at the St. Petersburg airport know of our mishap.

We didn't realize that there were two sets of friends trying to help us out. We spent days out of the now truncated week in Russia, cordially visiting with folks I have only seen a handful of times as a child, but who cleaned their homes and cooked for hours and bought us presents to celebrate our arrival. We were treated to many a potlatch. We toasted, and we ate. We barely spoke of my mother— a plumeless bird.

How do birds perch just so to grab their holly berries without getting stuck, without getting cut by those razor leaves?

× × × ×

Back in St. Petersburg the waiters and shopkeepers and museum workers mused: "That is a curious accent you have. Where were you born?"

"I was born here but left for America many years ago."

"I don't think you were born here. Where are you *really* from?" the lady at the checkout line says back. I buy some museum souvenirs and hang my head, a passing plague in her fair city.

For most of the time back in the town where I was born I tried to get up before noon and failed. I made myself wake up early to go to the American consulate to ask for advice on finding a relative who wasn't listed in the phone book and was given a shrug.

I sat on the curb outside every official building in St. Petersburg that may have been relevant to my search and groped for tissues in my pocket as meek as a granny with a runny-nosed kid by her side before getting up and riding the metro to the Hermitage for relief. The museum fortified me temporarily until I resumed my wait in fetid rooms to eventually speak with a police chief in my mother's old precinct who offered me a candy from his desk drawer after I offered him a sizable bribe. Still, no Elena.

The accidental spilling of salt is considered to be bad luck, so you must throw a few pinches over your shoulder to break the spell, to create the performance of control, to tip the scales of helplessness. Liquid salt has no way of being tossed aside.

I went to the city archives to ask after a recent death certificate or a wedding license that matched my mother's name and was told to leave by the elderly secretary behind the glass partition. She looked at my American passport and murmured that "Gypsies can make any kind of fake document they wish nowadays with computers." When I insisted that I had a blood relative who spent her whole life in this city and I came from far away to find her, she pointed to the security guard, who told me to lower my voice and exit without his help. I turned mute.

During a downpour, my boyfriend, who had long black curly hair and olive skin, ducked into a phone booth. An older gentleman knocked on the glass and gestured for him to get out, as though he had to use the pay phone in a great hurry. As my boyfriend scrambled to join me under a restaurant awning, I heard the man mumble: "That's right, black ass, step aside."

I did manage to visit our old haunts in search of you. The woman who lived in my granny's apartment had cancer. We spoke of God. She felt bad for not having more to say about where my family had moved to when Granny sold her the place. She confessed that she wasn't going to call me at first but the letter I left on her door had such careful cursive and that moved her to action. It ended by saying, "Please help me look for my ma." I did want to tell her that my hands weren't steady enough and I just dictated it to my father's friend, who indeed has perfect penmanship, but refused to unnecessarily disappoint her with the truth. My Russian letters are crude. But my instinct toward forgery is right on.

This woman told me that my granny also had breast cancer. She didn't get out of bed the day the sale was made. Her second husband did all the talking. Granny likely died shortly after the sale, as she had stage four cancer and looked dejected. I took out the cross I wore for the first time in my life and planned to gift to my granny and we lowered our heads. I didn't know how to pray.

× × × ×

"Look, it's little Sonia. The girl from next door came over," said the toothless woman to the man staring at his glass. The barren room had blown-out and charred sockets, black soot crawling up the walls with hanging wires, and a table with a bottle on it. They shook their heads when I asked after my family. I couldn't go inside, and no one had invited me to in the first place.

Walking away from the toothless couple I saw that if I leaned any further down to reach for you I would fall. But the falling was always the inevitable outcome of my looking for you in the first place. I landed right where I belonged, back in the place of not knowing, of Ma.

× × × ×

Sometimes on this trip, dissociating, I would pretend that instead of you being the missed and missing one, it was me who had to be mourned by you; there would be a story in a newspaper, our faces side by side, about me pitching a tent outside of your door, waiting until you came out and faced me, but I get suddenly struck by lightning instead:

The sizzle-in-the-pan sound lasted for hours while the torched girl moaned. The mother began vomiting two days later when the bubbles popped on the red-and-black tarp of what was skin. The mother asked why the body remained unmoved for days and was told it had only been fourteen minutes since the incident. She was told to sleep, and she slid in her daughter's place and stared at the blighted canopy. She woke up and was informed it was the same day still. The authorities insist on cremating the burnt remains at once, for the child could not be made to look human for a casket. The mother took her daughter's coal of an index finger to outline her own eyes; no mirror was provided. The girl used to be in and out of her, and now others can see her looking back as two black holes.

XXV

My boyfriend went out to explore my city by himself when I was too despondent to leave our little flat. He was a photographer, constantly snapping pictures of every event from his own point of view of an exotic world of Soviet-era leftovers, Lenin statues and young girls who lived in Stalinist buildings much like my granny's flat. He didn't take a picture of my granny's apartment or the toothless couple next door. These were not monuments, or works of great art, or relics of the past. These things were still breathing, too hot to touch, even with a lens. He had an ability to hold you from a distance.

With only a few days left in St. Petersburg I decide there's nothing left to do but to play hostess to my companion. I would take hot baths in the algae-green water after a sleepless night with a towel on my eyes to keep out the amorous light, mocking me, and attempt to move about as though walking in peanut butter.

During one of my restorative walks through the bedrooms and sitting rooms of the royals, whom some of my ancestors were indirectly responsible for killing off as soldiers in the Red Army, I overheard a tour guide tell a couple of Americans that the upholstered walls in the palace are a replica of the originals, which could not be salvaged after a fire. I was dismayed with this forgery because for most of my childhood I worshiped this elaborate silk wallpaper as something ancient and belonging to a decadent era of kings and queens.

I made a joke to the tour guide that they need to tell the kids who come through here that these are not original silks so that they don't waste their imaginations on the wrong fantasy. She pointed to the elderly couple in front of her and scolded me for rudely interrupting their private tour.

When St. Petersburg was still called Leningrad, *private* was a dirty word, and I hadn't adjusted to this new place with its new rules in the week I hid in museums on our native soil to think about you in the only way I have managed to find useful.

I found a room in the attic of the Hermitage where restorations were taking place. Everyone seemed to be away at lunch. A small canvas, a landscape full of yellows and browns, was in the process of getting its supposedly original colors back.

The window was open onto the square as the painting dried in the wind coming off the river.

What kind of data was collected about the state of the painting when it was still fresh? The restoration could only attempt to fix the piece up to a certain point, about the time one would begin to suspect the onset of an unacceptable kind of ruin. The larger, understood decay, had to be respected and drawn around. Once the new paint was applied, did the artist wait for it to dry enough to do violence to the uneven surface and generate new cracks for posterity?

x x x x

Before we went home to New York, we had dinner with my father's friends in St. Petersburg one last time. It had become apparent that I would not find my mother and the trip was a bust. I went down to the car to fetch a large sack with the fake Chanel purse, tube-rose perfume, lacy black underwear, and other goodies I had stashed away for my mother. They appeared embarrassed because the intended never showed up to the altar and accepting these things would be like wearing a used wedding dress. To change the subject, they spoke of the Russian skinheads and nationalists who wouldn't leave the Central Asians alone. They imported exotic fresh herbs and vegetables sold fairly, yet their produce stands were constantly looted. "Oh, the animals," my dad's friend said, glancing over at me protectively.

Before I left for Russia I had watched a video of an ethnic man from one of the former Soviet Republics being beaten almost to death. He looked like my father. They let him live long enough to make him watch his passport being burned. "Now you don't exist," a young boy with corn-silk hair in a buzz cut says, holding up the flaming photo.

My boyfriend began eating meat for the first time since childhood on that trip. Being vegetarian is quite difficult at a Russian table without starving and appearing rude. When we spoke a few years ago he told me that he still eats flesh to this day. That trip sealed his appetites.

XXVI

You used to be my fictional painter and my fictional painting. On the plane ride back to New York I accepted the recurring image of you with giant headphones hugging a glossy brown bob while you plugged and unplugged cords from a tangled wall of sound. Telephone dispatch operator on the night shift was the only real job that I remembered you had. I was beginning to arrange the details I previously ignored at will, a composition with the most potent of gaps, the chasm now echoed back to me.

Ma is a place of silence, a resting tone, a crater in between giving up and looking again.

Marcel Proust never reduced his dependence on his mother. As a child he religiously insisted on kissing her good night multiple times before finally dozing off, no matter the circumstance or her availability.

He wrote about ruined relationships through his fictional characters in drawn-out sentences that put others to sleep. He sabotaged his actual love affairs to avoid having to compare any intimates to the holy image he retained of his mother. He wrote for her and of her so breathlessly that to break up the kisses of each thought with periods would have corroded the unsettling wholeness that his mother provided for him. Proust lived happily within his nostalgia, where his lovers could never reach him.

I don't want to admit that the lover I chose at a time I could barely read a map was lost to himself. A lover who was coarse and unforgiving. A lover who left his jacket, with the return ticket to America in the pocket, on a bus out to our terminal. That he curled up in a ball in the corner of the terminal when the airline tersely told him he would have to purchase a new ticket. Nothing surprised me about Russian scams at this point.

I don't want to admit that after he screamed about how much he hated himself, refused to look at me, and told me that he deserved to be left at the airport, that I should run to catch my flight, I maxed out my credit card and bought him a new ticket.

I don't want to admit that I didn't even go to my old building, as

planned, to make sure my mother wasn't magically back there; to re-
trace the steps of my grocery errands, being sent to check for movie
times at the theater next door, or seeing my first two pirated American films: *Fletch* and *Midnight Cowboy*, shown in our cellar on a tiny
screen we paid five rubles to watch, or the newsstand where I fetched
my mother her cigarettes and scanned the front page of *Pravda*, pretending I was an elegant grown woman with brown leather gloves, a
periwinkle-blue scarf, and a smart green wool coat with a wide belt.

× × × ×

I don't want to admit here that I didn't find her—that I failed.

I don't want to admit that as your epigram I would continue to roam
free.

What is an epigram? A dwarfish whole;
Its body brevity, and wit its soul.

I don't want to admit that I wasn't alone on this trip to Russia, as I
secretly planned all along to be, before everyone talked me out of it,
so someone I loved enough to bring with me watched me crap out
in every way.

I came back with a suitcase full of excellent Russian linens—every
part of me hollow save a vulgar smile to bully and kick away the urge
to scratch my Soviet skin off and bury it, sit shiva for it, reenter society as teeth and gums only.

× × × ×

After a late shift at the shelter in East New York I was held up at gun-point in my apartment building. It was my twenty-sixth birthday. My photographer boyfriend and my best friend, Kelly, were waiting for me at home, just two floors up, so we could have a quick weekday celebration with takeout. The man who tried to steal my purse had a mask on and I could see only his eyes. He looked sad and panicked and I stared hard back at him and screamed until Kelly opened the door and he ran away. Kelly suggested that my boyfriend pick me up at the train stop for a while and his eyes widen; he feels horrible but thinks I can take care of myself.

That night, in bed with my boyfriend, with whom I felt a cer-tain kind of desperate passion—like a cheetah attacking a water buffalo—amplified by him being monotone and withholding, I talk about my mother. About feeling like my body is in another country and my mind is stuck, flipping over like a broken tape deck. I feel him drifting away and he is passed out when I look up at his face. Soon enough he will break up with me, too young to settle down, needing more experience, not sure being attached is for him. I don't blame him. And know I should have picked my girlfriend's love over a guy.

A month ago, he had returned from a tour with his band, but the distance never shrank. He had to leave almost immediately after we got back from Russia on a reunification mission ill-conceived and poorly slapped together.

Building bridges is a nauseating job of defying altitudes and measuring for symmetry and I chose the wrong pillars for the beam.

Since we had met in college on the day of our mutual arrival to A dorm, my best friend has offered herself as a mother figure to me, but I didn't take her to come find my mom with me. I wanted to go with a guy who moved to New York from Olympia and held me naked in bed and with whom I practiced being good, like a real couple. And real couples meet each other's families. Real couples take their partners back to their childhood homes. He wanted to see what Russia was all about. We were Cold War babies staging an adult version of a foreign exchange trip, but with sex and romance and restaurants. Our frontal lobes had just barely grown in and we were going to travel like lovers would. Finding my mother may have been the excuse, but it felt like a side job.

× × × ×

I don't want to admit that when we got back home and he left for tour I got drunk and cheated on him; that I lied about it when he found out; that I would later date, marry, and have two children with the person with whom I did the cheating.

Mother dear, will you kiss me good night?

XXVII

This is a new dream. You are an armless, white marble statue found at the bottom of the sea, the cracks slimed over by seaweed and barnacles still holding on to your torso like the hands of a small child pulling at the hem of a silk skirt, legs locked into triangles and butt sticking out for more leverage.

You were once sculpted and polished smooth, and came out screaming mutely in the image of the unseen and unknowable goddesses above. You were once a most greedy of guesses. For now, you are still the bed for the blankets of ships rubbing their bellies on centuries of rubble. For now, you continue to be lost out at sea.

When you're fished out, you will go to your proper place in a museum to be admired by me only. I will polish your bronze name plaque, and I will be writing the small paragraph, printed on heavy card stock in a tastefully solemn font, about you as a priceless relic, a found shard, degraded, a puzzling piece of history. A head lost, bust found somewhere, a battered woman with blank eyes, erected by those who had infinite worship in their hearts.

People like me "more easily accept that this beauty, so remote from us and lodged in museums rather than in our homes, should be a dead beauty or a beauty made of fragments," Marguerite Yourcenar writes of ancient Greek statues, restored to their "true" shape when fashionable and then broken up again to create a sense of authenticity. Most of these martyred and tortured-looking white stones, infirmed, castrated, and limbed gods in our museums, aren't Greek at all, but are Roman replicas of the originals.

Some damaged goods are items that were expected to be in good or brand-new condition but were discovered to be poor, tarnished, or already open, a fragment of their original form.

The Hermitage suffered a great loss in the 1980s, when I was old enough to remember the missing painting. A mentally ill man attacked Rembrandt's *Danaë* by splashing sulfuric acid on the canvas and cutting it twice with a knife. The streaked and torn-up nude lady in the painting was eventually restored and is now on display behind armored glass.

Goods are damaged often by no fault of their own.

All found art seems to go through four stages, much like the women in my family. Excavation. Restoration. Preservation. Forgery.

Nadezhda told us war stories, mined our family myth. Her daughter, Galina, kept us fed and ran the house. Her daughter, Elena, they tried to keep alive, even if just for show. Her daughter traced this lost image in her mind night after night, attempting to carve out a mother figure to imitate.

Studying a tiny crumbling picture secured by a piece of packing tape will not make a lost mother reappear, will not make her meaning easier to read, will not make her less ambiguous.

My other grandmother, Chaya, who was terrorized and brainwashed in Baku into becoming a stalwart Stalinist, believed that walking barefoot or sitting on cold surfaces, like marble, was unhealthy for the womb and could make you barren. Exposing any part of your lower torso during winter can swell up the kidneys and give you mysterious vaginal pain.

Every time Chaya observed me sewing she warned against leaving a loose needle around lest I step on it and it be carried straight to my heart, sucked in like my insides were a shower drain. I was instructed to always leave a thread with a knot on it after each use. This way she might be able to pull it out, wrestle it out of the river rapids of my veins.

Grandma Chaya worshiped Stalin the way one would worship a furnace repairman in a frozen town.

Stalin's wife shot herself in the heart before their daughter turned seven years old. Svetlana is asked by her mom if she knows where her soul is. She is told that she will locate it when it aches. Svetlana recalls her mother drawing a square with her pointed finger on the right side of her chest and being instructed: *that is where you must bury your secrets.*

Svetlana Stalin ran away to America with hopes of finding anonymity but came back to the Soviet Union in 1984 only to leave again a couple of years later. Her brother drank himself to death at forty years of age. She was not so much drowning but building rafts for inevitable storms. Water, water everywhere.

Jane Jacobs says being a victim is *rather wicked.*

Upon one of their joint visits to our flat, my maternal and paternal grannies argued over the best method of healing the sores I developed from being left too long in soiled diapers by my mother. As the rancid white cloth was boiled in a gigantic zinc pot on the stove they played tug-of-war. Granny Galina brought over a box of powder to keep me dry while Grandma Chaya thought the stuff poison and insisted on iodine baths. It was a soak I needed. Water heals all.

I used to wet myself while doing scales at my music teacher's house. I couldn't ask permission to go. I wet myself when I held hands with a heavily decorated veteran with gold teeth who came to greet the children at my school—I felt his war.

I would wet myself onstage during a school recital wearing a light blue silk dress and a gray scarf a teacher gave me to cover up the choke marks on my neck. I played a cloud dancing in the background and held up the painted cardboard to cover up my blood-shot eye. I would wet the bed at boarding school and cover up the sheet with yellow and brown rings marking the previous nights like counting the years of a chopped-down old tree. I slept in the wet and walked in the wet like before, always like I was still with her.

There are mornings when I hear my name, and it's your name, too, so I want to refract it back through my own porthole and keep lying here in bed, miserable, defiant, gone, and begged for. I want to be like you some mornings and only wipe my own face and ass and later be worshiped like a Greek statue by my hopeful-but-weary daughter. I want to drink here in bed until my piss warms my legs, long enough to make me shiver in the sameness of your river. I want to step in you twice as you run over heavy rocks.

XXVIII

The first time Mike asked me to marry him was before we ever had sex, the night I cheated on the photographer. He was firm and resolute, and I needed to be swept away, a blue moon, a full moon on a balmy August night in New York, bathed in someone's liquid courage and anointed with their amorous, cavalier, and childlike fortitude. I wanted to live inside a giant blinking YES sign every time I saw him and lick the wires. We had animal sex, ravenous, move the bed, hands punching the air—abandon wilder than what I had ever known.

He was soaked in urine—he thought it was hilarious to piss his pants in the street after a bartender eighty-sixed him—and I gave him a blow job anyway. I was going to consume and worship his body's wastes and gifts alike.

In the morning, when the deep remorse and hangover picked at my rib cage, I asked him to leave. I scooped his curls with both palms and kissed them. If he had stayed I would become her. The drunken whore my parents described. If he left I could pretend. I could still change.

The photographer boyfriend came back from his tour, from which he seldom called or wrote, and asked me if I had slept with Mike and I lied. He made the choice to believe me. All of his friends, our friends, saw us leaving in the cab together, fingers out of sight. They were the ones to pick up the check after Mike ordered expensive champagne to toast our engagement; the cigar ring held up on my finger only if I made a fist. They knew what had happened. But pretending was closer to the truth for me then. I pretended it didn't happen and everyone went along with this plan.

After the Fall of my birthday mugging, the photographer and I had a sad Winter. We walked through the dumb orange gates at Central Park and fought, broke up and made up, until he just didn't want to come back from our newest break. We were in our midtwenties. We were having a boring crisis. I knew we couldn't have had children together and so there wasn't much of a future to fight for.

I couldn't stop thinking about Mike. About corrections. About throwaways. About knowing a man, a tall, quiet, handsome man, with a huge Jewish nose and a German crooked mouth, a gnarled front tooth, calloused hands, elaborate hangover cures, silences so long they felt like dignified torture, distance like buried treasure, all mine, it was all mine to be had if I crawled for it.

I begged Mike to go out for coffee with me a few months after the photographer dumped me. At first, he said, "Why should I go out with you?" But I kept him on the phone and he relented. After coffee we had drinks, followed by goofy dancing and a trickle-syrup walk to my apartment on Ten Eyck. His chest smelled like clean laundry and David Bowie records and good manners and shyness with women and suddenly ancient drunken hookups and flowers growing from a crack in the asphalt and Marxist lectures and trips to Mexico, and our children. I smelled our future children's dandelion scalps shedding in the bath all by laying my head on him.

I wanted his scent and his bear claws and his German children inside of me.

Five months went by until I got scared that I couldn't commit, or that I'd lie again, or I'd cheat again—the hallmarks of Gabriel's grievances with Elena. And he said, *I give you my word, I will not tolerate you straying.* And I said, yes, I need this line. This rope space feels grand. I'll have this man, because nothing has ever been this urgent. Because after I couldn't find my mother back in Russia I only had the drive to make life where mass graves were dug up in my body.

× × × ×

Two enormous shoulder blades poking out of a Barneys tuxedo days before the wedding—chalk marks, adjustments to be made, the tailor smoothing out his back has made a bed for my face. My head on his giant shoulders. Amen.

The first time I got to touch my future husband was when I broke my ankle doing karaoke on New Year's Eve and he carried me down Avenue A on his back so we could keep partying at The Cock. I had not yet gone to look for my mother. The photographer boyfriend and I were doing well enough, but he didn't offer to tow me around, and I had always had a crush on Mike. I knew I'd get something potent from that contact. I never felt more skin through two big winter coats. I couldn't go home if he would piggyback me around like this. I ordered champagne and put my foot on the bucket of ice and watched him dance.

I understand the party-girl mom. I have battled the need for escape, the need to flee, the need to be unchained from a dyad, the need for a loud and raucous night that ignores the nuzzling rays of daylight. When I think of my mother getting dressed up and having a good time is when I have managed to carve out a safe space for my loss. I'm a party girl, too. I even have a matching tattoo with my two closest friends, in cursive, that says so. I can understand wanting a good time to last forever.

XXIX

I'm forced to think about what I believe in through being forced to think about what others believe in. I believe in fear. I didn't even want to drive until I was twenty-seven. I had been in enough car wrecks. A wise woman once said in letters, "I only worry all the time, I worry about my cervix, I worry about my uterus, I worry about my pleasant vagina and that reading too many books by women about things will turn me into an even more unbearable crank than the cranky poets who write hate letters." Bernadette Mayer's breathlessness is a hand on my stomach and pumps air into me.

My husband taught me to drive in the months before our wedding.

My girlfriends remarked on how strange it was to see me behind the wheel of a car when I was taking them to the rehearsal dinner. They vaguely knew about my fear of dying in a car crash and the actual crashes I had experienced. Of how my father threatened to plunge us into the next pole head-on if my stepmother wouldn't stop arguing a point with him or admit to her mistakes. The Camaro with the graying black paint was low to the ground and so loud that I could never hear what they were both upset about. I burrowed deep into the back seat and held my head, ready to roll with the car, imagining it would flip over, if only from the sheer force of his rage and the tension of her pleading.

My future marriage: we are driving. You are in awe of the mountain. You say the sky behind us is crazy. "Yes," I say. "It's on fire." I barely look in the rearview mirror. It's exhausting to be alert to the reds, to try noticing beauty, commenting on the heat when cold inside. I wish you would stop pointing out my blind spots, but that's how you end up getting hit.

A friend of my father taught him how to cause accidents for insurance money without harming anyone. We would drive around affluent neighborhoods in Philadelphia and wait for the gardener to step out onto the road, unrolling his hose, and brake very suddenly in order not to hit him. Then I had to get out of the back seat and hold my neck, moaning.

We had to keep on doing this until all of the elements worked out just so. Later we would see a Russian doctor who was in on the game for the physical therapy that took mere minutes. I was just as embarrassed at having to act hurt in front of strangers as I was at how long it took me to exit the back seat of the two-door. The seat would stick and not roll forward, so I straddled it awkwardly and pushed my chest through the too-small crack, all the while squinting my eyes in the sun, demonstrating distress. It broke my concentration and I feared losing my nerve. I wasn't asked to come on these trips after the first successful one. And I was never seen at the physical therapy office where I stared down at the shoes squeaking around on linoleum after my impotent X-ray.

My stepmother was scared of driving also but my father forced her to do it right. To practice. At night. Blue-black. Rainy. A kid in the back seat is holding her head. Lights. The woman pleads with the man to take over for her on the highway like Band-Aids ripping off. This won't hurt, but if it's fast. This won't hurt, but will take off some hair. A bald patch to remind you. Air it out, window down to heal. A sucking sound of glue doing its job to keep. The tires go . . . Strip. Strip. Strip. Strip.

Wassily Kandinsky asserts that yellow is the color of life. It is also the color of a deep bruise in its final healing stages.

She gets them home to the brown-shag apartment above the Meineke shop by the abandoned field in West Philly. He tells her to never doubt him again. See, we made it?

White is blank, but not always a fresh start.

× × × ×

Wedding planning is usually mother-of-the-bride domain—her chance to fawn over her grown daughter amid rows of froth and fantasy. With my original mother missing from the picture and my stepmother and I cycling through our perennial breakups and makeups, I had run out of mothers to summon for this occasion. And so, it was my father who came to my final bridal gown fitting after I braved all the busy and condescending shops in NYC and settled on one that felt safest within my feminist guilt.

Dad walked into the place to much bewilderment from the all-female staff, save one deliciously dainty older gentleman, brushing away snow from the lapels of his long black leather coat and hugging several copies of dog-eared *Russian Bride* magazines with neon-colored sticky notes manically swaying up and down as he approached the back of the salon. All of my girlfriends were sitting around caramel velvet chaise longues facing mirrored walls that reflected back champagne flutes illuminated by soft lighting. We all glistened and moved through the room like orange peels squirting fragrant oil on a flickering candle.

My dad got to work quickly, and within minutes the staff had all somehow begun hovering around him, looking at pages of pouty Russian girls with heavy lip liner showing off feathered and jeweled princess dresses of all sorts. I had picked out an off-the-shoulder cream duchess satin full-skirt dress with a nipped-in waist. I wanted a modest, or at least, less delusional, version of the gown Audrey

Hepburn wore in one of the final scenes of *Roman Holiday*. My hope was to find something elegant but plain—no lace, no embroidery, no distracting details, no sparkle, to be sure.

My plan was to eventually offer my wedding dress to my daughter or to my son's wife to do with as she pleased—the foundation was to be completely unassuming, inviting, and of sturdy quality. The fabric being a luscious cream color of timelessness, the already antique sheen inviting of wear and tear. The lack of embellishments would allow for a free pasture to roam, offering a springboard to launch her own path and mark that road map as she wished. Or cut the cloth to bits and start fresh.

The shape of the voluminous skirt was to be the abundance from which she could draw experience, expand or contract with the seasons. If my children and their spouses saw no use for it whatsoever, I planned on cutting off the ball-gown skirt, dyeing it a royal blue or lemon yellow, and belting it in with a crisp white men's button-down shirt. I would wear this to my child's wedding at the Brooklyn Botanic Garden, if they found it as enchanting as their dad and I once did.

The dress got sleeves, the sedate neckline was embroidered with rosettes of crystals, and the cream cloth was swapped in for a pure snow-white. A second version of the dress, designed by my father and edited down by me—a symbol of our feuds becoming paranoid handshakes—was cut and sewn anew by the perplexed designer, who delivered it barely a week before the wedding. The wedding itself had to start late because my father left his freshly starched tuxedo shirt with onyx buttons and cuff links hanging in the kitchen, miles away in Connecticut, and had to run over to Macy's to buy one off the rack in the middle of our broiling-hot photo shoot. In his speech he called on Mike to make a successful man out of himself within ten years. "I have lived in this country for fifteen years before I achieved my goals, and since you are from here you get a head start to make my daughter happy."

Gabriel values competition if it yields a secure and abundant outcome.

The way my father taught me to take my medicine was by stacking pills on his tongue and swallowing without gagging. The sheer number was impressive and showed me what kind of stuff he was made of, what I must copy in order to not get lost.

XXX

Mike and I were wed on Memorial Day of 2006. War made festive.

Eight years later on that date I drive to Olympia for a reading I have scheduled. Every bridge incites a pins-and-needles riot below the belt.

I had originally hoped that my husband and I would leave the kids with his folks and celebrate down there with all of our friends, the cartilage of our contact and connection getting worn to the bone. We had only recently moved from Cannon Beach, from lingering isolation and suspicious gazes of a coastal life in a watery bell jar.

Our daughter suddenly gets sick and so Mike stays behind in Portland to care for her. I try to get my two best friends, Matt and Sarah, to come along with me. I want to get drunk and forget with them instead of memorializing my marriage, but they have to work and can't come. They were my family before I married and birthed my way into a new clan.

I drive to Olympia by myself and listen to the radio. The first story is about a missing plane, Malaysia Airlines 370:

> DR. PAULINE BOSS: One of the first things you want to tell families like this is that what you're experiencing is an ambiguous loss. And it's the most painful kind of loss there is right now because you have no assurance of the fate of your loved one. And then I add this: it's not your fault. And I add that line because most people who suffer from this kind of loss tend to blame themselves. I should not have told her to go on this flight. I should've gone on this flight myself instead of her. All of these kinds of things go through the minds of the people left behind. And so, it's very important to tell them repeatedly it's not your fault.
>
> ARUN RATH: But when you have that degree of uncertainty, how do you know how to move forward with coping with that loss?
>
> BOSS: They aren't going to move forward right now. Right now, they're in a survival mode. Eventually, we hope, with family and community support systems that they can move forward. But the only way I found that families of

the missing move forward is if you allow them to hold the paradox that ambiguity causes. At one moment they'll say, "I think they're at the bottom of the sea." At another moment they'll say, "I think perhaps they're alive on an island somewhere." That is normal. That is natural and typical reactions from ambiguous loss.

The vanishing of this plane is considered by the news media to be the most bizarre and puzzling story of 2014. For the people who are still waiting on proof that their loved ones are actually dead, waiting remains the only story. Victims of the missing are now hiring private investigators. The disappearance makes no sense, like in a murder scene with only traces of cleaning fluid and no hair or skin flakes. The path to the missing is too clean to follow, but also too clean to let be, since it indicates someone took care to erase the person. There is no such thing as a vanishing.

Today new conspiracy theories about the Malaysia Airlines flight suppose that the Russians hijacked it.

The second piece of news on NPR is about the gang rape of two teenage girls in a poor Indian village who went into a field near their home to relieve themselves and were plucked from the tall grasses like rabbits, skinned from the inside, and hung to drip-dry in tandem on a mango tree.

The year 2014 launched the lunar tetrad of four consecutive total eclipses. The four Blood Moons. In some Christian circles this occurrence is a sign of an impending apocalypse.

The day after the reading I wake up late at my husband's friend's house. His old professor's wife is there alone when I come out of her basement. We sit in the kitchen and talk about babies, my babies and other babies she knows, always a danger with babies, always trying to keep them safe, keep them alive. "Next time I will bring them," I say, "for sure." Like a sack, babies are brought, or put down.

She makes me an omelet, bright yellow folds. My cholesterol is so high, I explain, my heart could burst any minute now. She takes a piece of fruit out of a bowl and says she has these delicious ripe mangoes that will fix me, they have what I need to cut the fat from my veins, and starts peeling the stubborn flesh with a dullish knife.

We talk and talk and I force two slices down my throat with a fork. My mouth is where I picked to be lost before and I will do it again. I will choose to be mute and not blind and not deaf. I can force my tongue to lick and roll around mangoes for now. I can't tell her about the giving tree and she hasn't brought up the story of the mango tree.

I have never seen a mango tree. I have never eaten a just-picked mango. I hate the word *ripe*. I can't eat mangoes, maybe ever again, maybe not until I forget about what getting hung from a mango tree means and that it will never end. When I come home from the Olympia trip I notice that I have mangoes sitting on the windowsill and the radio is on again and it says that my children shouldn't be in the room to hear this. I think I can let them rot, I hope they rot, the stupid fruit by the open, open, open window.

But my children are hungry, and I have a dirty kitchen and no snacks, so I cut them up. They are stringy, the juicy pulp. And the slices are thick, and the slices are wet, and they are making my fingers sticky and I can't wash my hands right this instant like I want to. And my son takes the bowl fast because he is famished, so they are in his mouth now finally making him so full. And the story on the radio is buried and gone. The kitchen is on mute. The fruit disappears. The children are fed.

I see skinned rabbits when I close my eyes. I see the giving tree's stump when I kiss. I see the mango tree when I fuck.

XXXI

Cézanne looked at the fields outside of his house intently. He stared at the fruit on his table until the color he saw delivered a fraction of its promise in layers of paint. Cézanne plowed his earth, tilled the wheat, and then gave it to the heavens by immortalizing his plot of dirt in oils. Much like a priest cannot take a vacation from believing in God, this servant of canvas and light could not afford to take a day off from painting, even to attend his mother's funeral. He painted *until his eyes bled.* It was in his fourth decade that Cézanne had become relentless and ruthlessly obsessed with his work. He was most nourished when securing a live model. He seemed to enjoy hounding women to come over and be still for him; their subsequent countless rejections only emboldened him.

Sometimes my dad brought home a white bunny and skinned it for dinner in our Leningrad apartment. As he held it up by its feet and tore at the incision by the tail the fur seemed to turn inside out in his other hand all the way to the ears in a single motion, exposing the pink shiny meat and the membrane in between what puffed out and clung back like second skin, like saliva bubbles popping from a baby's drooling mouth.

One of the more tender things my father did was pretend to be a bunny rabbit, sniffing in my ear and around my jawline, as though rooting around for food. He pursed his lips together and sucked air in and out fast and gentle. This was so pleasurable and exhausting. Most horsing around usually comes in the form of being wrestled, tickled *to death*, or thrown up in the air—our impulse for violence inverted. My kids beg me to roughhouse with them, sometimes until one of us gets pinched or pushed too hard. But the bunny breath always brings them back around.

My father accuses me of being an adamant prodder each time I mention Elena. He feels that I am married to my own blind truth and press him where he's too sore to the touch. That I don't know enough about our family and don't know "what enough is." Since I left home the day before my eighteenth birthday, we haven't had a visit that doesn't involve him calling my attending college in Olympia as the time I abandoned him to move to the farthest available state. "Ever since you ran away from home . . ." he begins the speech of filling me in while I suck on a pickled tomato in his kitchen. The words for *runner* and *refugee* are quite similar in the Russian language.

"I don't ask you to continue in my footsteps, but somehow you end up repeating my old mistakes," Dad tells me. He is referring to him becoming a dentist, an oral surgeon, more accurately, at what he perceives as a later-than-normal stage of one's life. Because he felt discouraged and unable to fluently converse with people on a deeper level in a second language and didn't have the chops to hypnotize patients in a broken English with a heavy accent that further inhibited him, he swiftly moved on from psychotherapy as a feasible path forward. When I was in high school he went to NYU's dental school for a career change that seemed most prudent to him, especially since they offered a program tailored to immigrants whose credentials were now all but useless. Dad has displayed the misery of excavating inside of and drilling down into cramped smelly spaces in his gorgeous black eyes ever since.

Bunnies must constantly gnaw on hard wood or their teeth will never stop growing and become too sharp and long, possibly unusable. That's what Franny's day care teacher tells me about their classroom bunnies. Their names are Smokey and Fire and they are often used as distractions for transitioning from tearful morning goodbyes. When I peel Franny off me and hand her over to her teacher I also wave to the bunnies. "Too hot to pet, huh?" I say, looking past them, to my daughter's red eyes.

When I was thirty-four years old and heavily pregnant with Franny, I had to have a rotten wisdom tooth pulled. I instinctively put Babes in Toyland on my headphones, Handsome Greeeeeeeeeeeeeeeee-tel . . . Babes, who wrote *Spanking Machine*, *To Mother*, *Fontanelle*, are going to the tit, biting the source of pleasure and rioting out and into their mama's arms.

I power through. The tooth they let me keep has a big dark hole and only one sharp root. "You are lucky," says the bone butcher. "Sometimes wisdom teeth have two roots, but mostly four, and that's much harder to extract."

There are four kinds of human teeth. Incisors for cutting. Canines for tearing. Premolars. And molars for grinding.

Inside my daughter's gums her adult teeth are pushing out the babies to be put under pillows and later stored in keepsake jars.

If I needed a tooth pulled or drilled as a child, my dad's empathy and frantic need to suck out my pain were fully on display. Dad would lie in the dental chair so that I could sit on his lap as he held my wrists with a reserved softness to get me to stop swatting at the buzzing instruments. He gave me instructions on dealing with the sharp ache and fear: to pinch, scratch, and squeeze him on the legs as hard as I could for as long as I needed to. He asked God to give him my pain. Dad believed in this transfer of powerlessness, that he could carry my load even as my own gums were ripped open.

All Russian parents recited this refrain when comforting their children after a fall or scrape: the kitty hurts for you, the mousy hurts for you, the doggy hurts for you, but you, my baby, hurt no more. They blew a kiss on the bruise and off you went, an animal able to project her pain onto other sentient beings without the means to defend themselves.

A rhino hunted for its ivory runs in fear of captivity. She knows not whether the gun pointed at her from the chopper is to kill her or is a stun gun to knock her out and take her to safety. The animal only knows of being hunted. It only knows of poachers. The endangered rhino is surprised when she is in a new land being released. She is grateful but will never trust her new surroundings fully.

But I was the one who left. I parted. I divided. I conquered my fear of flight. Found my best byre to hibernate my explanations.

No matter how much my father hit me or called me a slut the way the kids in high school did, he wanted me to be someone, to make something of myself, to make him proud. He slapped me so that I would stop trying to be a person who'd fail at making him swell with pride each time he looked at me, talked about me, or thought about me, which according to him was often. Because we were of the same polarity, both given up on, with no metal to hold us together, he had to be my mother as well as my father. Because when she left, the loss of this magnetic center shifted our sense of direction. The needle caved on the dial and he went blind watching it spin.

He wanted me to sit in a vaulted-ceilinged library with knee-high argyle socks, pouring over law books, staring pensively out of a picture window as yellow leaves fell on a damp-with-dew ground in slow motion, edging limestone buildings covered in climbing ivy.

He calls me Sonechka, or Syustik—his nickname for me. Mostly, I am Sonia, the diminutive. Outside of the home, I am the formal: Sophia.

He often calls to tell me he worries about how I am doing out there and knows I could go farther still. His farther and my farther are not aligned. Father, we are not aligned.

The way mirrors are made of ghost mothers brushing my hair behind me as I stretch my arms out to tie a bow. That I came from what was gone before holding on could mend me and forge a shield against my father.

The way airports are made of blue canvas travel bags given to me by my dad's boss in Italy. In the leaving there is the memory of getting away and not dying.

The way high school hallways are made of boys I used to kiss saying I'm a stupid whore when I stop kissing them and get recycled into a rumor.

The way these boys would wait for me outside of school and throw pennies my way, yelling for me to pick up my worth.

I don't believe we belong to each other the way my father does, but I'm in the business of making the same polarities of magnets touch without repelling. I'm in the realm of the unbelievable.

He wanted me to know restraint and propriety. Those were only secondary to loyalty and a love of poetry.

I took his unyielding will to persevere and thrive, I took his ruthless stubbornness, I took his hunger and his yearning, I took his impatience to inject meaning and soul into the mundane, I took his unwillingness to accept injustice, I took his stanzas, I took his traveling legs craving miles, I took his brazen tongue, I took his blighted sense of self-worth, I took his conveyor belt of lovers, I took his tears on my lap, I took his chest-beating tantrums, I took the gem out of the stone of his eyes, I took his pounding fists, I took his waking to run out of strange beds, I took his berry-stained bruises, I took his bloodshot vigilance, I took his nails peeling back as they scratched and held on too tight, I took the ammonia whiff in the nose holding back liquid anger, I took his believing before seeing, I took his staying when he could have left and made it the gust of wind begging for speed at my back as I fled with his bad and his good.

When he fears that we have lost our center, Gabriel starts to tell me stories about my preschool years. I often came along to his night classes where I learned to be patient and funny sitting in the grand lecture hall. When his professor asked if it was time for a break I made a little joke to the class: *We don't need a break, we need to go home.* It went over so well that there were nights when the other students would wink at me or bribe me with candy to blurt out something precocious to throw the teacher off track and get them to early dismissal. Dad would leave the room to use the bathroom and come back to a cluster of adults watching me demonstrate how I crack an egg. He picked boogers out of my nose and told me they were as good to eat as my eggs were because I was delicious. He relished leisurely cutting my fingernails with his rounded scissors. He thanked me for my competence and stamina. *Moya somastayatelynay dochkah*—my independent daughter, he would beam. "Her favorite phrase is: 'I can do this on my own.'"

My dad seemed like the most gentle and loving man in that lecture hall, drawing me pictures and peeling my oranges while keeping one eye on the blackboard.

"I dreamed of having a father my whole life," he would impart, eyes that spill if they catch mine. "You get to have a father, and I wish I'd known what it's like to have the protective presence of a man around—an influencer. I used to lie awake in bed as a young boy, and dream that I was a poet in Paris, and imagined my father being proud of me. My mother never finished grade school and wanted me to fix watches for a living because it was a practical trade."

It was another outrageous myth about our uneasy dyad that I pretended to agree with, like his belly birthmark, which looks like the linea nigra of postbirth—see, I'm your ma—and him being able to reinvent the role of his own absent family patriarch while also successfully replacing my mother. His lack of a father and my lack of a mother was something that he tried desperately to bond with me over, but the hospital corners on the bed we made felt too tight.

XXXII

I found out the sex of both of my babies around the fourth month of their gestation.

There are four people in my family and we live on the fourth floor of an old brick apartment building in Portland's northwest quadrant.

I think preservation is a dead art, but I have the need to live in old buildings and wear someone else's old clothes, and walk in someone else's old shoes, and put pictures of dead writers on the wall above my desk made of old doors from a remodeled house I will never visit.

Because I decided to think about you, again, around the time I was pregnant with my daughter, I began to carry a picture of your face near me at all times in my wallet. Very soon after, I watched as my son took out this small photo and crumpled it up in his little hands, the gray dust flaking off and permanently creasing the fresh young facade. I ran toward him and took it away like they coach you to push the baby out, with steady, shallow breaths so there's minimal tearing. I hugged him to cover up the waves of resentment cracking my chest open; bit the violence into my own lip and left his body unharmed, circle bent.

I made an enlarged color copy the size of my head of my mom's photo before it was accidentally destroyed and taped it onto my dressing mirror. Right where my own head should be when I get in close to put on eyeliner like she used to, all the way inside, behind the eyelash—they don't call it a waterline for nothing—there's a missing persons poster instead. Inevitably tears come to the corners of my eyes and spit out tiny black balls of residue. I lack clarity and good vision. My chest holds a whale where only a goldfish could swim.

My son collects rocks, horse chestnuts, and twigs in his drawer. He hoards pencils and pieces of scrap paper he steals from school. They turn to pulp when I wash his things and fail to empty his pockets. The horse chestnuts aren't the edible kind and are poisonous if ingested raw. None of the things he collects can last or nourish, except for the rocks.

"Why does the sky look beaten-up-red?" Jake asks me at 7:00 a.m. "How did the sun do that?"

I still fall asleep with my contacts in even though the doctor instructed me not to. "The lack of oxygen will ruin your eyes if you keep it up," the Slovakian optometrist with twin daughters and good sense says to me at the fitting. I woke up on the couch with my clothes still on. My wrists have red rings from the elastic of my dress sleeves.

It's Mother's Day. I got really drunk with friends the night before. I feel like my teeth need to be swaddled and rocked out of my head. I can walk around and play with the kids by dinnertime and act right again "from now on," as I mostly had every day before I got drunk at the Florida Room, bumped my head on the photo booth machine, ate nachos, wrote obscenities in chalk on the pool table, and told loud stories about a guy I slept with a long time ago—before my husband, before the photographer—whose penis was shaped like a tuna can. I meant to say it was thick and short. But once the initial field report was out there I couldn't back away from my story and kept lying and laughing. It's been almost a decade since I had sex with anyone other than my husband. I'm not supposed to think about this fact as much as I do.

There was a guy in my writing community who came out for drinks after our MFA department's annual writing awards ceremony. The conversation turned to sex, to issues of promiscuities and double standards. I explain that I still identify with slut culture, with hyperboles necessary to call attention to the lingering shame and imbalance, the safety concerns women continue to have. "You can't be a slut, you're married. The word for you is just horny," he scoffs. When he said this staring at his beer, he looked like a mean, proud, lost baby bear that I wanted to hate-fuck, but never would. He reminds me that I have animal skin. He reminds me of the stickers in Seattle. He tells the table of writers he will be moving to Chile to avoid paying back his student loans.

I tell him that I ain't ever leaving. I love America. It's broken, like me.

What if the name of the town and country you were born in changed after you left? What if you lived in three different countries within a year right before you hit puberty? What if your native tongue had to twist to shout new sounds, trying to touch the top of your teeth to say the word *teeth* in front of a classroom of predictably cruel seventh-grade girls? What if the only word, the only name, the only place that remained constant was Ma? Mama, mama, mama, said so many times that it broke off and became half of itself, just Ma, no breath left to give to a whole word, so you speak the end or the beginning only.

When putting my daughter down for a nap I try to leave the room and avoid the creaky floorboards like I'm navigating a minefield. Frances will scream by the time the door handle is turned anyway. I lie down with her, contorted into the best feeding position, and wonder what it was like for my great-granny during the massive shellings in Leningrad.

If she thought about making little earplugs out of newspapers or the hem of her dress for her little daughter to keep out the noise of approaching doom. But maybe those scraps you would need for kindling. I want to sew earmuffs for my baby so I could leave her in peace for a few hours, but never get around to it, and so she suckles, and I dream about the war, about Hope's stories, about the names we give eliminated things, eliminated people.

Nostalgia. Shell shock. Battle fatigue. PTSD.

My daughter screams out my name every morning, our house rooster: Maaaaaaaaaaaaaaahmaaaaaaaaaah! I swing out of bed like I'm throwing a punch with my whole torso to greet her sweaty bangs and part them to the side to see all four of us—me, you, your mom, and hers—staring back against the stream of the light coming in behind me.

Frances has almost Inuit eyes, extra puffy in the morning, igloo-melting browns, and I watch her stretch out on the writing desk I made into a changing table, the letter and envelope compartments holding diapers instead of passionate correspondence and magazine submissions. I wipe away the poop that smells as many different ways as you can say *snow* in that cold language.

I think about how I want to be her so badly. I want to feel myself stretching with no memory of pain in my muscles, no reminders of where wood once met the small of my back on dad's bed; no slap on the back of my neck that stings when I roll my head from side to side after he comes to my recital and realizes I have been only pretending to practice the violin in his bedroom and instead looking at his Japanese anime porn mags by laying them out on the floor and flipping the pages with my big toe as I fingered the amber-powdered strings in dissonance. Amber preserves all it traps when the resin's still wet.

A violin is shaped like the daughter, a higher-pitched cry than the cello, the bridge also notched with four strings, head rested to the side to play a song by heart with a horsehair bow.

Toward the end of my extremely short and unproductive violin career I told any adult who listened that I had a big wish. I prayed that my father would become a very rich man so he could keep buying violins and I could keep breaking them over the backs of chairs. Violins against women no more.

When our car is broken into again and again, Jake cries over his stolen backpack. Smash-and-grabs are so common in Portland. I teach him that someone must have been so unwell that stealing from us was all they had left that night and resorted to crime to survive. But his backpack had homework and favorite talismans, his sacred nothings. Why couldn't they have left behind what mattered only to a child, he wants to know?

We find a man asleep in our car. He's covered himself with Frances's nap-time blanket and has put all the stuff he wants in the front seat. I failed to unpack after a camping trip. He is dope sick. I try to open the door and a singed hand with browned fingernails slaps the lock shut. Franny cries out, "He's touching my blanket." When he finally leaves I'm holding the children in my arms and tell them that he needs help. The car is full of Gatorade bottles half-filled with his urine.

Jake bit a kid at school after weeks of unrelenting questions about how our family would survive an earthquake put him on edge. I tell him that he cannot bite others. Or scream, or say bad words, or run away, or interrupt, or refuse to eat, or slam the door. We must follow directions. We must be patient. It seems that he knows from watching me that I used to love doing the things that have earned him a time-out. That I learned not to do them to others first by doing them to myself until nothing was left of the chewed-up spots and a new way had to be found. He will eventually ask me about the scars on my arms and why we don't see my folks very much. For now, we look at each other and he knows about the other way. Say sorry and give a hug after you take a pause, after *ma*.

Moments later he yells at his little sister, "Give it back, no fair." Always wanting what he could have if he waited. But the desire is too enormous of a geyser. Because waiting doesn't guarantee a reunification with the thing you gave up, even for a moment.

New friends tend to ask why or how I chose to become a mother after I out myself as so elaborately motherless. I had to stop myself from looking for her, I explain. Not the looking I did on the page, counting every eyelash on her gloppy mascaraed eyes with a corresponding letter, but become too busy raising children to go back to Russia again and be dissatisfied with the search and its outcomes. I didn't want to travel for pain anymore.

If place is a language, then without countries we would be a new kind of poetry. We would be a wall of lockboxes and a bowl of un-numbered keys.

XXXIII

I have been pregnant four times. Abortion. Miscarriage. Baby boy. Baby girl.

I have given away. Been taken from. Mother. Mother.

I learned that in the summer of 1940 Anaïs Nin had been selling pornographic stories to pay for an abortion and support herself in America after fleeing Paris. Against the backdrop of the Nazi takeover she remarked on her own survival: "Each pregnancy is an obscure conflict. The break is not simple. You are tearing away a fragment of flesh and blood. Added to this deeper conflict is the anguish, the quest for the doctor, the fight against exploitation, the atmosphere of underworld bootlegging, a racket."

Sappho is believed to have been writing a feminized version of *The Iliad*, while the men before and after her penned war torture porn.

Each time a soldier leaves for active duty they number her tours. By the fourth deployment it is usually expected that the soldier won't be sent to a war zone again in her career.

Before I had Jake I miscarried suddenly, within forty-eight hours of telling everyone I knew. I sat at home bleeding with the dying, or dead, fetus still inside me when the balloons, flowers, and teddy bear delivered from my father showed up at the door. I knew I was done waiting, done rubbing progesterone cream on my thighs, done expecting it to pass like a red fog in the toilet bowl. But I couldn't do anything but wait. In the middle of the night I felt like I had to bear down on a toilet. I saw two black dots on a puppy-like head in a pinkish sack maybe four inches long. I asked my husband if I should keep it. I wanted to bring it to the doctor. Get it analyzed. I wrapped it in clear plastic, a body bag that I put in the freezer.

The next morning I went to the new doctor I had begun seeing only months before the miscarriage. She wanded me with the internal sonogram device and declared me empty. She then asked me about the ancient white scars on my arms. She was concerned I wasn't stable enough to handle this miscarriage and was at risk for self-harm. I told her I did the cutting when my mother died, which was a lie.

Didn't she? Did she? It only happened a handful of times, but the forearm is the worst place besides your face to have that kind of flaw. The last time I cut my arm I was turning twenty and I never got the urge again. I remember the excuse I gave the gynecologist I never returned to every time I am forced to put on a cardigan in the dead heat of August, like the time my daughter got baptized.

Franny's dress didn't fit at her baptism, so I left the back open with its buttons untended. It was a Victorian-era find that was better on a hanger than on a nine-month-old baby. The sleeves began to rip before the oil-slicked thumb traced a cross on her forehead. Her purity further heated up being held in my ugly, thatched arms.

As soon as Franny could speak in sentences she asked, "Did you ever have a mother?"

I let her stay up late one night and we look at my old photos. We sit on the edge of my bed by a dim lamp, Jake passed out beside us, another night I give in when they persist about sleeping with me. "Cuddle us all night," they coo, and roll over, kick, and rub their faces into the cold part of the pillow away from me shortly after their fevered pleas.

Franny holds my pictures carefully, asks questions about locations, about my outfits, and then suddenly begins to let down a tear. She wants to know why I'm alone, standing in the courtyard of the Vatican. Who's with me? I explain to her that Grandpa Gabriel was my constant companion, but I was taken from my mom. That she wasn't well, but that people live on inside of us, through stories, mostly, or so we tell ourselves. I don't want her to take care of me, take my job, take my place, but she slides right in, right up to me, and says the impossible.

"Is she living on through me?"

While I'm on the phone with a friend the next day, Franny interrupts me to interrogate the scars on my arms, the ones I can no longer notice or pay attention to. I put her on my lap and tickle her tummy, but she calls me out for avoiding her question. I lie and say I got them in a car accident. "What kind of car accident were you in, Mom?" I hang up with my friend.

× × × ×

The reason Anaïs Nin needed a "Lie Box" in her mature years was so that she could organize and catalog all of her different selves into a neat and predictable order. A stoic and lush portrait could form out of a stack of impressionistic sketches she practiced on her friends. Each of these cards held the evidence of her mind's intentions to become whole, to fill in the blanks where she was left empty. To have written herself out of the freezer, to turn gruesome tiny body bags into precious keepsakes, proof she survived a stolen childhood. My scarcity *and* mercy role model.

Anaïs gave birth to her diaries instead of children. She proclaimed motherhood "a vocation like any other. It should be freely chosen, not imposed upon a woman." I chose, and I didn't. My mother's leaving picked this for me the last two times I had gotten pregnant.

I signed a contract to not re-create her and showed up for active duty armed with a toy gun.

It is in me to leave my children. It is my destiny to make them unhappy. Those are the roaches scurrying around my mind when I turn on the lights in the kitchen of the proverbial house my mother built. When my mother drank instead of continuing to nurse me as a ten-month-old, she cut away at the stable and confident future-mother-me; I got annihilated as a natural, as the real deal, as her truest, most important poem, her Lie Box. But she stuffed some torn-up papyrus in a crocodile; she taught me how to look for shards of a vase with a few words on it and piece together a story. She gave me the words when she gave me up. She passed down an invisible language I am learning to read each day and transcribe to keep as naked proof that you can live without heat in your house. Maybe you can survive motherlessness.

My dad often scolded me for losing my mittens as a child. Rubbing my blue fingers in between his palms, he looked into my face and repeated, "Cold hands, cold heart." I stick my kids' hands into my armpits and tell them this story while they try to tickle me, trapped for a moment.

Soviets believed iced drinks caused viruses and flus. Drafts caused pneumonia. A chill on the back brought on spasms. A neck with no scarf made for a sore throat. Sitting on the frigid ground caused women to become infertile.

Scientists say that there is no such thing as cold; there is only the absence of heat. It's not that our houses get chilly, it's that we open doors and let in a draft, allowing the warmth to escape. Do I make my children cold when I leave this apartment to write, to get a drink with friends, if I'm hungover after a fun night out, if I lose my temper, or spend the night lying awake and going over a perfect day of inhabiting a studio apartment with nothing but books and a television and no kids around? Do they feel the chill of all the wide-open doors my mother left ajar within me? Am I freezing them out when I write down what my life would be like if I never had them?

What if I never made them dinner and cleaned it up and washed them up and begged them to get dressed to get undressed to go to sleep to please wake up to stop yelling to wait just one second to not be angry that I have to go now to ask their father that question instead to not rip the book out of my hand to play quietly to not wipe snot on your sister to not be afraid to be patient Mommy is on her way and I will cuddle you on the couch and yes we can watch a movie and forget the books the phone the friends the vodka soda on the rocks and sneaking a cigarette and cursing with my best friend walking around too drunk to button my coat in the winter and forgetting, forgetting, forgetting my body ever held them tight all to myself and my mother's body did, too, and doing it all again at 6:00 a.m. the next morning all while something inside of me is snowing over the road back to holding hands while crossing the road together and missing her too much to go on.

And so I only leave them for a few hours to write about her leaving for good. And I write about her ghost to find my wrung-out skin—to feel my lips kissing my children's necks, bellies, hands, feet. Touch as worship. An altar of my goddess with her broken-off nose and no arms to take a drink of wine. Marble took me for its daughter. She needs fresh flowers and ripe fruit instead of roaches and lice. A divine blossom from her assimilated fruit.

Restoration is the act of finding a baseline to maintain.

I make jokes that I should have had my tubes tied. My friends who hear this wince a little. They know my kids are loved and well cared for. Each one planned out and fretted over. It sounds calloused. It also sounds beautiful when you say it out loud. Tied tube. A knot. A bow. Like pinching pasta. The twist on the dumpling. Closed off and sealed. Like an envelope. Unsent letters living and dying inside your canal.

But it is also a noose, which is finite. And I am not—finite. I birthed two children. The wish for the noose under my skin has to do with me being a sieve. I'm not a funnel for my offspring. I try to protect them from the larger bits of truth. Chew them up myself before letting them swallow. I'm a round meshed device that is constantly trying to strain against the familial history of cheating, leaving, drinking, and fists swinging for faces. I know what I inherited. I know how hard I must work to protect my kids from the matter already in their marrow. What I fed them through my placenta and my milk and then sometimes the lost and sorry look in my eyes no matter the smile. The tiny jabs of beige on my arms pointing to them, don't notice me, I'm too visible. I wished for the closing off of two holes inside of me to not infect them with my mother and father at their worst.

My children are contaminated even though they hardly know anyone on my side of the family well enough at all.

I haven't found a way to teach them my mother tongue. "Oh, but they must learn a foreign language, especially if their mother speaks fluently," a well-meaning poet once said to me at a reading. I lied and promised that I will. She is right: only the young have the ability to master new tongues.

× × × ×

"I always tell my kids that you were the golden child," Luda informs me one winter when we are both grown women. I'm still not supposed to call her a step. It's a siren call back to the missing one. The one she calls a prostitute within earshot of my kids. My reflex is to say that *prostitute* rhymes with *substitute*, the way I would have when I was a child, but she needs me to say less, not more.

To her, I'm an appalling elegist of limbos, provoking spectators, for shame.

In Doris Lessing's *The Golden Notebook* Anna is a divorced mother who keeps four diaries, Black, Red, Yellow, and Blue, because she "has to separate things off from each other, out of fear of chaos, of formlessness." Anna eventually harvests the jumbled recollections she organized and compartmentalized into her "golden notebook," a prisoner no longer dusting her cage.

She bleeds. She fucks. She breaks down. She reintegrates.

And so did I as tarnished, fake gold, a changeling underneath the paint. The person I grew into displeases my parents. I'm too angry. I don't take making money seriously. I have no solid plans. I live too far away. An abandoner. A coward. An infidel. As though there were a battlefield and I fled without dragging other wounded bodies to safety. A runaway, still, after all these years of them hoping I was somehow forging anchors in their basement apartment in Brooklyn, still a stray thing, which can't be petted to stillness. Dock here, they say, but I see no land in their faces. They scowl and look at each other when I explain that I'm settled in Portland. My stepmother cries and wonders why I reject them, why the miles between us. What is it that I'm looking for in a city they can't pronounce and have never visited? Will I ever stop running? I was abducted by *her* in the end to be sure.

Leningrad, Lido di Ostia, New York, Olympia, Seattle, and Portland are all port towns where I have continued to wait on a sinking ship, on a lost parcel, on a body to be sewn into canvas and sunk to the bottom of the sea like in a proper naval burial, seeking her out to the exclusion of all other parts of my life, never asking for directions, rejecting quaternity.

The Greeks did not portray the Sirens as sea deities but as meadow creatures *starred with flowers*, who loudly lured nearby sailors with their enchanting voices to shipwreck on the rocky coast of their island.

By the fourth century, the Christians discouraged belief in sirens.

This Lie Box is a trunk stamped with your songs: Baku, Pushkin, Leningrad, Vienna, Rome, Philadelphia, New York, Olympia, Seattle, Cannon Beach, and Portland.

XXXIV

Now that I am a mother, I see my two closest friends—Matt and Sarah—about twice a month. We try to get a lot of catching up into as many vodka sodas and cheap beers as we can. The night always costs me an extra day and an old lesson. During one of these outings, Sarah playfully told me that my daughter can be a tiny terror, which is a term I have used myself when she wouldn't sleep. She is my kids' godmother and her sarcasm is harmless and meant to be supportive. She sees that I have been wistful and hard on myself. It's difficult for my family to go away on trips with our friends; it seems impossible because everyone has to be quiet when the kids are asleep early in the evening. Our schedules are different. I have been pretending otherwise to not get left behind, even though I'm the one who moved ahead in her eyes.

I walk home from the dive bar sucking steam and repeating "I have children" over and over. I don't wish to fear my blessings, but I warned you, I'm a Believer, too. The only religion that's left for me now seems to be motherhood, performing the ritual of the unseen, hovering spirit above me.

What happens to people who are born into a fate of instant adulthood; who are molded from the get-go to be self-reliant and then a caretaker? Their eventual resentment creates the chaos of not finding the right escape hatch. You can either be a child in the beginning like you should have been or become a child when the ticket for that ride expires. The former is not up to you.

My dad told me that if I ever get too drunk—and I shouldn't get too drunk because I might end up like my mother—but if I do get too drunk, I can make myself throw up. He said it to me when I was stomach sick, and I was sick to my stomach quite a bit as a teenager with what the doctors said was a bacteria called *H. pylori* and took rounds of antibiotics to cure with no avail.

I might have been pained in the gut by the absence of a mother. This mother—I was told from the time anyone can remember anything so frightening and simply put—was no good, and a drunken whore.

When I was sick to my stomach as a child, my dad would take me over to the bathtub in our Leningrad communal flat. The toilet and tub were in separate quarters. He said that he didn't want me to throw up in the toilet because it's dirty to look at, and you need running water to drink. One needs running water, to take little gulps and cool off your wrists as you rinse your hands to properly throw up. He explained that he would be putting his two fingers down my throat and all that has festered in my gut would be gone, and I could sleep afterward.

You need to get all the poison out, girl. If you ever drink, and please don't, you should just make yourself throw up like this . . . and you will feel better.

Sour cherries stomach. Stained pits.

"I never stop believing that I am loved. I hallucinate what I desire," Barthes proclaims of his conquests, like a spoiled brat, always a mama's boy, inserting her into all of his affairs with an insistence that he mattered more in rejection than in acceptance, because the thrill of the chase held his interest like a rascal aiming for birds with a slingshot.

× × × ×

Sarah, Matt, and I are what they call in China the three friends: Plum Blossom, Bamboo, and Pine Leaves—holy and noble; these hardy plants survive the winter.

Matt and I met in Seattle. He used to scurry home from cheating on his boyfriend while there was still cum on his hoodie, maybe even a variety of strands. He was a spank bank, crawling into bed with his nerdy soon-to-be-lost love. I would come out wearing only a towel from the room next to his and say hello, but we rarely talked about anything back then. We were not best friends, yet. I just happened to be this fast girl that his roommate brought home. Matt thought that I was full of sass and freedom, so free that I constantly forgot to put my clothes back on after having sex with J and only managed to wrap up in a soiled towel to use their bathroom.

J was my only boyfriend to have shared his sexual abuse history with me. We had the same knotholes. He shrunk, and he shrunk like Alice instead of taking his shame out on women. I spent many nights in his room trying to console him, trying to get him to stop shaking, then helping him have sex with a steady hand and eye contact after he confessed that maybe he can't, but really, really wants to, because his dad had molested him. He's all liquid, inside and out. I fuck him back to solid form.

I keep doing this after we fly out to visit J's parents and hang around listening to Simon & Garfunkel in his old bedroom where he used to go soft before we met, where I kept his secret as promised and nodded to his dad when he asked me if I want seconds of dinner, but tried to never look him square in the eyes. I then made his son feel better again because he can finally get it up, because he finally got this out into a safe deposit of a girl.

Maybe he was sprouting glossy fresh leaves on dead wood, but did he know how I liked to fuck? Not like the giving tree. Not like the giving tree at the end of the children's book. Not like the giving tree in the children's book in his childhood bedroom where his dad hurt him and now sits in the living room watching *Letterman*.

Matt thinks he knows how I like it. Maybe this guy or that girl thinks they know. Sometimes they were strangers and sometimes they were old customers at the peep show and sometimes they were friends, but rarely were they people with whom I was intimate who asked how I wanted to be touched, or knew what to do with me.

"I thought you were more of a whips-and-chains-dominant type. You probably rule in bed and spank your boyfriends," an old friend wonders aloud, and then tells me that she loves pulling a cucumber out of her fridge and maybe finding a hole for it. She makes a fiddling gesture with her hand and says that she likes it when her husband cums inside her. "No, no, no." I shake my head and make my mouth stretch hard against the *O* sound. We both laugh because I am overly direct, yet still a bit of a prude in her eyes. I can see the things that grow in the ground and how they go in the fridge and then my friend's face as she cums safely in her bed with the man she loves. I'm grateful for a new schema to internalize.

Matt, Sarah, and I go to Seattle. At home I leave behind these small children, ever-growing, unlike fruit in a basket. It seems like they go all over the house as they please, as they should—diapers get full during meals, diapers come off behind the couch. I get to watch them, smell them, and wipe them, and that's a blessing that they can do this near me, instead of in a rape field. I drive away with my two best friends to Seattle to party, to temporarily not wipe them while my husband does double duty.

We call this trip, which we have taken many times before, The Boner Jams tour. Like hot guys tour as bands of boners, we tour as those who would jam these boners, who listen to these boners jam, who collect stories about hot boners—our own tour. We are boy-crazy and love rock 'n' roll. It's a weekend of satire. Matt and Sarah are single and can flirt with boys without much drama as we visit our friends up and down the I-5 corridor, always Olympia, always Seattle.

I can only look, and so I only look. Maybe kick the can down the road. I visit old boners. My old boneyard. The harem of my ex-boyfriends scattered like the contents of an urn along I-5. Bars, bars, bars. I meet their new girlfriends. They tell me about the breakups and I listen to their new plans. I meet their fiancées, who tell me about managing the brewing wedding chaos.

I want to cum, but the TV is on, and bridges over troubled water, and the giving tree, and the mango tree, and cucumber seeds, and pulp, and ripe, and dirty hoodie, and greasy omelet, and hole in my back, and at least they had each other, and cut-out tongue, and sticky hands, and my son's empty orange bowl, and I'm looking and looking, and the bone yard, and it's back to that tree on the radio.

XXXV

The national anthem used to blast from the mounted radio every Monday morning at 6:00 a.m. at my father's Leningrad apartment. I fell asleep to that radio, one state-run channel that went to dead air at midnight. It was ostensibly my alarm clock and parent to get me up for the long commute to boarding school.

I will listen to the radio when I arrive in America and Prince eggs my right hand on to slide inside my pants. I stop turning it on for years. After Mike and I are married he flips on NPR every morning while making oatmeal and it becomes my habit, too. I will listen to the radio while cooking breakfast for my kids. I like to play this game of chance and switch around channels on my old Volvo's stereo with the rickety tape deck. I mute it every time the words *rape* and *murder* are uttered if the kids are in the car, then hold my breath temporarily, hoping I didn't traumatize them, but still needing to know the whole story. While I pop a Quasi, KARP, or Bikini Kill tape in to distract them I mumble the details about the segment, so I can look it up as soon as we get home. How many ways can it really end?

Whenever men sing love songs to women on the radio I don't think they are for me. I picture myself as the guy and I'm speaking directly to my mother. If the lyrics seem sexual I bypass those words by humming and concentrate on the need, the want, the chase, the absence, the raw and base desire to be one with another. This has nothing to do with fucking. It's about symbiosis.

Before loneliness will break my heart, send me a postcard, darling. How can I make you understand, I wanna be your woman.

Sappho was a lyre player, a singer, an accomplished musician who was summoned to serenade important weddings and grand parties. She ran a boarding school for girls and threw elaborate graduation parties to see them off on their new journeys as artists, philosophers, and musicians. She sang freely about women and love because in her time platonic relationships were celebrated as much as sexual bonds.

Your basic hot rock star.

Out of sheer necessity—being called a slut by girls who didn't realize we were provoked into a dogfight, bets placed, nothing to be gained—I would evoke my own rock stars. Women had already lost watching the Rolling Stones instead of being them. Who would sing about women like my mom? Why aren't there like five thousand songs about heartbreak over your drunk mother, instead of dumb boys and breakups? What if that's the real reason your heart hurts?

How come there aren't more songs about losing your girlhood to a nasty troll? Or more sad songs about losing your best friend for the first, second, third time to a pack of piranhas who play guitar, tell you to take it easy, and never call you back?

× × × ×

In Olympia, the riot grrrl movement asked us to share our skills, reassured us that there is enough shiny stuff, enough ephemera and magic, for all to go around. That we should puke it out if we are nervous but get up there anyway and take our shirts off in the pit when we get sweaty at that show. Radical honesty and vulnerability in art were not only genuine acts of revolt, but also served up a tongue-in-cheek posturing and agitating tool that was pleasurable and political, a teasing, bratty kind of taunting, a deadly serious game of hide-and-seek.

Olympia is where I met Penny Arcade—the woman with the heaviest swinging balls of steel—when she came to the Capitol Theater to perform her *Bitch! Dyke! Faghag! Whore!* show. I ran backstage immediately after she sang, danced, and monologued through a skin-peeling performance and found her gathering up her props, sweaty. As a typical New Yorker, she had her belongings stuffed in a white plastic grocery bag, which dangled on her right wrist and now swayed back and forth with my sobs like a buoy out at sea as she held both of my hands. I found my place with her in that moment, *unspeakable*. And then I immediately ran away. I went home and fell asleep in the middle of the day, seasick from becoming known so wholly for once.

A mother by proxy to many lost girls already, Penny didn't kiss ass or hold back her tongue; mercilessly candid rather than odious, she made art alongside the Warhol crowd, the 1970s punk scene, the gay liberation movement, and the various junctures of feminism. A goddess to girls who walk around with a scrim of missing with a capital *M*, not just a certain someone, but a life less stiff, organized into neat piles of success and failure. That was longing we were experiencing, not nostalgia, said Penny. We don't ache for an imagined utopia, but are livid over the theft of our friends, identities, cities. We are allowed our anger over this lost pavement, the scrubbing out of the families we made away from our own. That urbanity is to be worshipped, because we runaways want to be stacked and slapped together while having the solitude and space to reinvent ourselves outside of claustrophobic homes built by anxious immigrant strivers. Maybe we are staring at and dwelling on a sinkhole where we think our vanished people might be, where our cities might be, but Penny is unsparing in her approach; her lack of nuance is refreshing. She'll give you the belt, buckle side out. Through much loss she recognized that we can choose interdependence without the masks, our mourning within the collective. You can't break off her pointed finger, you can't balance and meditate and belly-breathe her out.

She birthed the hot feminist artist, the conundrum of the Valley girl genius, the one who doesn't fit into what's considered smart or understated—she wants to crack jokes about French feminist literature and smoke weed and have sex and demand to come first and then take up space in a way that keeps flipping what brainy women are allowed to do and look like on its head. She is sad in her valor, refuses to wipe noses. I'm thinking of Chris Kraus being called an egghead intellectual, a soft-boiled critic, of Chris herself, calling Native Agents, which she edits, "the dumb cunt" imprint of Semiotext(e). I'm thinking Karen Finley here. You accused the megaphone of whining, but it's catcalling you back, baby. This girl-woman with sometimes "fake" bravado and the stains of thrown tomatoes on her see-through dress reinvented and launched by fourth-wave feminism—the movement of my youth—to live on in the literature of the future. The motherless future, the auxiliary mothers future.

× × × ×

Amy Fisher is being pushed and pulled through the crowds in handcuffs. Her long, wild, wavy hair is draped like a curtain of shame in front of her face. Her baggy white T-shirt is tucked into light-blue frayed cutoff jean shorts. Amy is walking very fast and it's sunny and breezy outside. The wind forces her shirt to cling to her barely-there breasts. The hair in front of her face makes it hard for her to see where she is going and so she holds her knees together like a grasshopper and leans back as she moves rapidly toward the courthouse where they will sentence her to jail time longer than they would ever consider cumulatively giving to all the men who paid money to fuck a child, or took money as a pimp and lover of a child.

Valerie Solanas thought Andy already had the guns and the bullets and the army and the horses and the whole damn war room. She was the smart coward who didn't bother challenging him to an actual duel. The lesbian prostitute writer, excluded by the girls she wished badly to impress in Andy Warhol's glamour art army, shoots the general. She was pushed around and laughed at because she was *ridiculous*, power hungry, and yearning for the undying affections of all of these hot and stoned girls she wished to mobilize. She was ridiculous because she wanted to be Andy Warhol, and there was no other desirable script, no Valerie Solanas yet to be.

Garbage is as garbage does, the jury says of Aileen Wuornos. When I'm watching the fake rage of boys screaming in bands I think only of Aileen's real rage. I would take away their stage and give it Aileen's familiar anger instead. Her palms are red from sleeping in the snow-covered woods as a girl. On the video screen, where she now lives, Aileen raises cuffed wrists to her neck and fish guts seem to spill out onto my lap. Herring, herring everywhere, but not enough to eat.

Amy Fisher becomes a mother and writes a book about this new meaningful life as a caregiver and citizen recovering from her haunting experiences of sexual and physical abuse in prison. She is hoping that family life will save her, launch her into a new realm, give her peace, make her whole *again*. It sounds like a postscript. Like her life had already been lived with Joey Buttafuoco and now she is healing from the grave, dirty fingernails and no soap. She's never going to stop being involuntarily douched by the media, by us, by the memory of him.

Wounded girls—some ripped open for you to see clearly, some hidden and left in the ditches of a battlefield we don't dare notice. After reading the headlines about the impact of Malala's new book, *I Am Malala*, in the paper one Sunday morning when I am heavily pregnant with Franny I stare at the wall and imagine what it would be like to be shot in the head, and have a yearning horde of competent adults wanting to take care of you, root for you, talk about how smart and special you are—your life made precious by tragedy. It is not so for girl prostitutes, for the Amys and Aileens and Valeries. What it often takes for the world to think that girls are important is a bullet in that freedom-loving, precocious brain of yours. These would have to be the right kind of girls, though. Don't pretend you don't know what I mean.

In this daydream I'm lying there, of course unconscious, as English doctors work on my injury, the beep, beep, beep of my heart steadied by a pump, but I'm really fully present, watching myself from above. This happens because I've read and have seen video footage of my rescue. The chemistry and the narrative of trauma are completely altered by what you are told had occurred by witnesses, and then retell in the days, months, and years after the event. That's how you can make something up and believe it for self-preservation, or think something real is made up because it is way too much to have actually lived through.

My name is Gretel, yeah; I've got a sloppy slot. I am an Aileen with a father who cares to keep me alive and schooled. I am an Amy who didn't fall in love with her daddy, her john, her pimp. I am a Valerie without more Andys to humiliate and use me. I am a mother to a girl who will stand on all of our smeared shoulders, some that can't be brushed off. Franny will have object constancy, her own revolution, her own potty mouth, her own army.

XXXVI

Right after Franny was born, the elementary school shooting happened in Fairfield County, in Newtown, close enough to where my half-siblings live to obsess me past my limit. I watched it on the hospital television as the glue-wet baby head bobbed for the ripe apple of my tit. I was told to concentrate on my lovely, helpless child and turn away from the gruesome news of children shot like fish in a barrel. I found a way to let myself mourn when expected to be jovial.

Home with the baby I listen to the radio as always in the mornings. The news of the gang rape on the bus in India rolls through every forty-five minutes. The girl dies from severe internal injuries.

My womb is shrinking and draining itself of the blood that cushioned my daughter onto witch hazel–soaked pads I intermittently grab from the freezer. My pelvic floor muscles inverting back in like the rope of a tire swing pulled over a tree branch. The bed is a swamp again.

I leave the kitchen and walk to the laundry basket. My husband reminds me that this is my time to rest. I do not recognize the meaning of the word inside my body or mind. I reach in for tiny pink pants and my lower back seizes up and I go into spasms, flopping around on the oak floor. My back goes out in the same place where the frozen fish was once placed by my ass crack, where the wood once met the bone. I remain on the floor for days nursing Franny, padded by pillows, Mike changing out my soiled underthings.

To whom do I owe the woman I have become?

I bind my torso right before Christmas and use the wall to learn to wobble-walk again so I can make it to the toilet on my own, but mainly to be the kind of mother who wraps presents and makes a lamb roast and has friends over. A hostess who can't pass up the chance to play against type. It's not enough to heal and be available to my baby, I must also create an atmosphere with the smells and sounds above and beyond the nuclear family. A love buzz a pitch higher than what I had the gall to aim for in the first place. My youthful fantasies at the Kirov Ballet, not the damsel in adult diapers eating takeout on the floor with out-of-town friends excusing themselves to leave early.

Four weeks postpartum, I take my newborn to class with me in January—Elena's month—refusing to skip a beat. I nurse Franny with the reliable left breast and take notes with my right hand. I know what I must look like: a beast. Or a woman not suited for certain public spaces. The baby spits and farts. With her gummy flesh strapped to my chest I wiggle out of my Velcro back brace to go pee, to change the giant pad. I change and reswaddle her. I bring up Solanas's SCUM Manifesto in between tending to our bodily needs, and the discussion about humor and erasure infuses my daughter's milk. I can't stand the silent milk of staying home.

× × × ×

Mary Ruefle, Agnes Martin, and Emily Dickinson were born to worship art only. They are born in our eyes. God knows what they really worship. Maybe it's something that stuck in Catholic school, maybe a tree, maybe aisle five at the Goodwill before it gets picked over, maybe a special kind of off-white paint and the grids it etches into the brain and then the canvas. But that something is definitely The Voice, their own or God's, or rather the joining of the two and the ensuing dialogue mushed together like warm stool in a diaper, the kid going down the slide, arms up in the air, ready for more at the bottom. It must come. It's pleasant and scary and necessary.

Ruefle called her process of writing poetry having to "go pee, but in your brain." The room where she announced this lit up at this statement. It was wonderfully childish. She was serene and sublime. She was goofy and deadpan. Naughty and nice. Poignant and casual. You want to be her to be yourself. The snakeskin found on the road might give you shelter for a while until you find your own way.

Here's what I know: I want to be Ruefle, but my son has been accidentally soiling himself at school nonstop for at least three weeks now. Leaks everywhere. He is diagnosed with encopresis.

I tell my husband that the same thing happened to me when I was a child. "How long did it last?" he wants to know, half concerned and half unable to hear what I am about to tell him, which is that it lasted for most of my childhood. I held it all in and then I spilled it out, bit by grim-youth bit. It's a disease, having to go like that. It's not like having to pee very badly and it's only in your head like for Ruefle, and bless the Lord, it's a poem. It's the thing that stops the poem. Encopresis trumps writing deadlines. I want to pen my own Soiled Dove Plea in defense of that smeared girl.

I break away from my writing desk again and go to the elementary school to bring my child home and shower him. He's crusty. He's embarrassed. He can't seem to stop himself. I can't write like this, not while my boy suffers. Everything smells like I'm too small to write. And in small there was death; the potential to be vaporized from the waist down.

I think poetry is in the rectal canal. I think it's in your pelvic floor. I think it's in your sphincter. It's in your anal glands. Are you stretched out? Are you sore? Are you bleeding? Are you comfortable? Do you have to go? Do you know when it's time? Are you indeed pleased with the world down there? I would rather have a knock on my head that says I gotta go, and out come the words, but I must hold words back. I want to say monstrous things, speeches I have heard in a stomach frightened like a body bag. I want to ask why, and can you smell yourself and how did this happen to you, and is it because it happened to me?

Chris Kraus says, "It's all fiction." Once you type anything, once you say anything, make a speech, a show of yourself, it all becomes a made-up tale to tell, and all attempts at finding proof become scratchy recordings of gossip—multiple holograms.

A poem is knowing when to go, if you can. Sit up straight and deliver.

× × × ×

A guy sits next to me, too close, even though he's far enough, at Powell's coffee shop where I seek escape in between nursing sessions to write about conceptual art made by women. He is staring at me, staring at my piles of books. Yoko Ono's *Grapefruit* is at the top of the pile. He looks like a lot of hot guys around my age who don't give a shit; who are really deep, but would laugh at that sentiment; who smoke a ton of weed but don't seem to get that high because they are always hovering above the smoke; who look dirty because maybe they are filthy in the sack, or "loving" in an almost too wet of a wetness when they get you into bed, or, most likely, they make you get them into your bed because they never want to try hard at anything.

And they know, they must know you are rigid and coarse and see right through them. They want the opposition for sport but expect submission. They will tame you and find your mellow side in the end. He asks me, finally, leaning in, if I'm a writer and what kind of stuff do I write, what kind of stuff do I read. I say things that I know will turn him off. I have two children. Not enough time to be magical. I'm trying to get him to go away without calling the police of my siren-blaring mouth and my eyes, onerous and slightly ridiculing when he says that he loves Rimbaud, of course.

He borrows my Ono book and gives it back too soon without a word. I say that I mostly like derivative and autofiction writing by women. I begin to fantasize that planes are landing and leaving from the bookstore and that he's now getting on the wings. I hallucinate his departure, my static descent.

This scene here has happened to me so many times before in other coffee shops or bars or on buses or whatever public area I sit in and try to carve out my own space in the world while fearing I'm taking up too much, taking on too much. And the guy there, here, everywhere is ripping my seams open with a tiny little penknife. Can we have the envelope, please? I'm glitter spilling out. He hates the show.

As I approach forty, the number of men telling me to smile, cheer up, to not look so sad, is getting smaller. As my tits sag and the bags under my eyes point to my sagging tits and the glimmer in my eye says I have been there and done it too many times already with no variation on the theme's outcome; the more my body and its language express a climb to an age, a woman losing the girl, the more this happens, the more invisible I will become to this guy and to the world that loves Rimbaud and tits and smart women writing alone in coffee shops so long as they look unavailable and disinterested and busy and tight, above all, tight and smelling of spring.

Above all, spring.

XXXVII

It's around four o'clock every day when one of us must go fetch the children from school.

"Step on a crack, break your mother's back," Jake chants over and over at the bus stop, and jumps on me unexpectedly as I almost buckle. But I tighten my stomach where the doctors taught me to locate my core and hoist him up for a piggyback ride home. A man I frequently run into around my building asks me, in a cheerful and almost leering way, if I am the live-in nanny for the two kids he constantly sees me with.

Jake's head is all rye. Eyes of April fields and hair of fall harvest haystacks. He studies my dark olive skin and blue-ringed eyes. He rubs my black locks between his fingers, pulling at a foreign soil. When angry, his green eyes are rock quarry swimming holes, algae rage in still waters. I pet him with the grain.

Colors have a direction and a corresponding number in eastern numerology practices. The number for green is four.

My skin is somewhere between Russia and Iran. My father was born in Azerbaijan. He was the fourth and last surviving child his mother had. There are four countries that border Azerbaijan: Russia, Georgia, Armenia, and Iran. But there is an ongoing war in the region over a heavily disputed territory, so the borders shift their shape with blood and fire.

I check the "white" box on myself on our OHP application. I check the "white" box for my son on his kindergarten forms at Chapman Elementary. How can we be in the same box?

My son had a bris to honor my father's family. And so a fragment of his manhood was removed to be nearer and dearer and cleaner for God while I looked away and bit the side of my cheek. After nursing him to sleep I went swimming in my father's pool with all of his friends looking on in disapproval, as it was only about a week after I had given birth. I went down the pool slide with my younger half-siblings and waved at them cheerfully, chlorine and infections be damned.

Both of my children also had a baptism, because I imagined she would have wished for this. And so your grandson was dunked in a cauldron of cold water, chilly and clear like vodka.

I'm a traitor to no one because no side can have me. I could light a candle for my mother in a church, but I wasn't taught any of those prayers. I do know the prayer to light Shabbat candles, but I shouldn't have bitten that fruit, shouldn't have illuminated my own empty space. There is a word for fatherlessness—*bastard*—but what is the word for your kind of absence, one without a grave or a phone number to call?

I am unspeakable, as Kathy Acker was unspeakable, and I ran into the fire of others, for the gleam of light is a dry psyche, wisest and best, according to Heraclitus. The ancient Greeks believed that a wet psyche, a dampness in the body from drinking alcohol, made a person useless, foolish, and an outcast within their intellectual society. Mainly, it made you lose your direction and you followed people around inappropriately without any sense.

As a displaced root system too wet to live under your muddy soil I will teach my children about exile, helping their seedlings adapt to a drier climate.

× × × ×

Numbers are a way of arranging the chaos. Anxiety pieced out. Resistance examined.

Our primitive caveman stance remains, passed down stallion to foal; mare to colt. The human that lived in constant danger of snakes and bears invading his shelter was on the kind of hypervigilant alert we have come to understand as post-traumatic stress. Man was dying of paranoia. The real monsters were so terrifying and potent in the way they haunted his waking and dream life that he created phantoms to battle, myths and stories about invented creatures and bad luck. The notion of the evil eye, that someone can cause damage just by looking at you in a harsh manner, has carried on through centuries.

All Russian children follow a superstition about wearing your clothes inside out, because if you do, you will receive a beating. Your friend should tell you right away if your seams and tags are showing and give you a symbolic punch to ward off a real one.

If an adult has an itchy nose, they will be getting drunk soon. If a child has the same itch, they will get hit on the nose.

A person eating from or licking a knife will be possessed with anger like a rabid dog.

Opened bottles must be drunk until the liquor is gone. Empty bottles cannot stay on the table or be placed on the floor. There should not be a pause between your first and second shots. Latecomers to the party should drink a large penalty glass.

We believe ourselves to be castaways, abandoned by the gods, forgotten by the muses, lost souls, and that others in our midst have the power to channel these curses onto us. That we deserve harm for thinking about naughty things. That the darkness in us will be found and punished, or that we will simply fail to be born to the right person or be at the right place at the right time. That another human can cast a spell on us. That wishing harm is equal to doing harm. That curses shall find the cursed at last. That we need to be in charge of goodbyes while we still can.

A compass is a device used to determine direction on the surface of the Earth. East and West. North to South.

The magnetic compass, which relies on the fact that objects tend to align themselves with Earth's magnetic field, is the most common. My children love to watch the arm dart around in circles. There are other kinds of compasses that determine direction by using the position of the sun or a star. Some use a gyroscope, because a rapidly spinning object tends to resist being turned away from the direction in which its axis is pointing.

Early compasses were shards of lodestone on a piece of wood or a reed floating in a bowl of water. It was known that lodestone attracted iron. Eventually, a needle of lodestone was pivoted on a pin fixed to the bottom of a bowl of water. When suspended in gimbals, the compass remained level and was used aboard a ship being tossed around by the ocean.

Magnet a metal. Brace a neck.

Survivors of catastrophes are like deer roaming narrow pathways with a dart in their hind leg. When my children hit or pinch me it's like brush snagging the ends of phantom arrows. Rupturing more flesh where the meat grew around the wood.

The deer survives the predator, but it doesn't survive the effort of running faster than itself. Even with the lion finally left behind, the deer dies from her survival, too shaken to enjoy silence, always listening for danger.

Not everyone is fit to live with silence. That's what the protagonist in Marian Engel's *Bear* tells herself upon finding solace within a cabin on an island way out north, knowing she can't stay, reveling in the stay precisely because of the impermanence.

And you ain't gonna get lost on an island. But you can be stranded.

A shoal is an island without a tree. A body in the water with no root system. All mud and weeds. And you ain't gonna swim home in them winter waters, either.

XXXVIII

My daughter's doctor prescribed her a cream that thins out the skin on her vagina. It turns out that her diaper rash developed into a partial labial fusion. The body could turn into a swamp, the German pediatrician explained as she instructed me to hold her steady so she could pull her lips apart.

As she recovers, I read a lot of the books to Frances about lost bears or bunnies looking for their mothers. I'm cold, tired, hungry, and afraid, these babes cry to the moose, deer, or owl they meet on the journey back to their burrows and caves. Not a single children's book I've come across yet has the baby bear not find her way home, not see her mother at last when the tale is through—a failed reunification.

Like the bunny in the children's book, I had the runaway instinct early on. But I played both mother and baby in the story, hiding away and looking for her as though she were my wayward baby.

I teach Frances all about her body in the bath. I give her a warm washcloth and show her how to spread her lips to the side and not use harsh soap because it kills the good bacteria. "It tickles to wash down there," Franny discovers. We decide that *the button* can be very sensitive, and it is hers to figure out over time. Nobody is to touch her without permission. That only doctors and parents can ever see you naked unless you're at hot springs or the beach or you just feel like running through the field naked. I want her to run through the fields naked forever and ever if she wants to. I want her to know that her button means fire and ice.

Her brother is in the bath as well. He's paying attention to everything I say. I catch his eye and explain that his body is also sacred and important to explore in private. To remember that we do not touch other bodies without their consent. It would be like stealing, but worse, to do otherwise.

My mom once kidnapped me from my dad. He asked her to babysit for him while he attended an evening class at Leningrad University. As soon as he left the apartment she looked around for my green plaid coat with matted fake fur trim. But when she finished bundling me up, we heard the lock turn in the front door. She stuffed me in my cot and tucked the blanket under my chin. I pretended to be asleep. She sat on a chair beside me and her gaze seemed to glue my eyelids. He left again.

A few hours later we were on a train out of town. She held me over her shoulder and I stared at large jars of pickled tomatoes some old lady on her way to the dacha stacked next to her seat. I don't know what our final destination looked like, how long we stayed there, or what happened when we were forced to return home.

In the mammalian kingdom there are cannibalistic mothers, voracious mothers, vampiric mothers, and phantom mothers.

Rabbit mothers immediately leave the burrow after giving birth and only stop by for a few minutes each day afterward in order to feed the litter. After less than a month, the kits are left to fend for themselves. But the rabbit is actually protecting her young by minimizing the chance the burrow will be violated by predators.

A rabbit mother will freeze when frightened. She's a coldhearted warmblood, a creature of contradictions. The mother runs fast but knows that a still bunny won't be spotted, so when in doubt, she'll do nothing. When her wait becomes unbearable, it's time to run again.

The mother rabbit's efficiency astounds scientists, observing her nipples burst like grapes as she lies over the hole in the ground and squirts milk into the mouths of her little ones in about a minute. She promptly escapes the litter until she's too full to go on.

Nursing a hangover. Nursing a baby. Nursing yourself back to health. A hospice nurse for a body that feels like sponge cake left underneath a leaky sink. By the time my cup size reached the fourth letter of the alphabet I was moaning in the shower as the coarseness of my breasts would not turn soft. Every place I squeezed and popped the caviar-like collection of blocked milk more places had to be beaten into submission. They say you cannot choke or suffocate yourself because a mechanism in your brain is there to prevent that kind of self-harm. Your arms would yield toward survival.

My hands kneaded out the milk knots, lumped fat unmoved by my barbarity. Eject, eject, eject the baby's liquid gold. Drink a beer like the nurse advised, dunk the blue-veined bags of rocks in scalding water and try again to make it flow out. The cysts remained for many months. Rubbing my breasts in sticky ointment and packing them on ice before plunging them back under the hot stream were the moments when I saw that my path to motherhood wouldn't be reparative only. That I am to bite down hard on the hand that helps my son grow, now that I made myself plural. That I wasn't going to replace you this easily, or ever, that my breasts would ache without you, too.

Jake preferred the left breast, the bigger producer. He almost choked on the flow. The neglected right breast shrank and made less and less milk, proving the baby's point until I became extremely lopsided. Symmetry betrayed a woman who wants to live by numbers.

If you've had a baby, you might know what it's like having things that you were used to holding dear ruined until you learn to put *your* toys away. When they are no longer babies, you might know what it's like to have amnesia and miss those days. If you had a baby, you may know what it's like to have your period and hold your tampon in with your middle finger inside your vagina while you push out a number two. If you're a mother, you may know what it's like to do this while having someone screaming at you to get off the toilet and there is no one there to rescue you. You may then forget to wash your hands. This is still a Soiled Dove story, a mother trying to write holding one thing inside all gushy warm and the other thing failing to come out against all odds.

XXXIX

It's by the sink, and then by the record stack that I think of Cat Marnell. You don't know. You've heard of Cat Marnell? Sure, okay, but you do not understand how much she makes me think of my mother, how much I wish to protect her. The men stealing her fire and torching her like she is boneless and will vanish quickly enough all while she hangs on to their dear legs for life. Our connective tissue is stiff after a lifetime of men colliding into us, into our desecrated foremothers, the Connie Ramones, the girlfriends, the groupies, the support staff with a mattress, diving off barstools while the men we reared dove off stages. I put on an anthem to make the chores seem like theater. Turn off the radio show that goes on about our narrow approaches to sexuality: aggressively advertised or chronically repressed. They should try being the three of us. Choice like at a prison canteen. Choice from that deep a lack needs to be modeled and learned anew.

I get the dishes done. Lurch forward. I hate the wiping part. All the kitchen towels smell like last week no matter how much you wash and repeat. I fuck the forks up. I notice myself not doing it right, fighting with the egg yolk, but I'd rather wipe the crud off on my skirt when the table gets set later. I hate sitting down at a table to eat. I think about Cat Marnell when I do the dishes because I know she eats in bed, she eats off other people's plates, or she doesn't eat. If you don't use your body beyond the bare branch, the bloom is beside the point. It is for suckers to grow flowers, pansies like me, crossed off, cross-shaped like a lilac, doing dishes here while Cat Marnell parties, my kind of girl. It's insulting to consider my potential for danger here at the sink while Susan Griffin makes duplicates of echoes:

This is a poem for a woman doing dishes.
This is a poem for a woman doing dishes.
It must be repeated.
It must be repeated,
again and again,
again and again.

When I finally saw *Jeanne Dielman*, the Chantal Akerman film of my mother's nightmares, a quickening, like that of a first kick from the baby in the womb, tapped away at my forehead. Akerman used an actress of glamour and stature to do mundane chores for nearly two hundred minutes, famously peeling potatoes long enough to bore you into nausea. But you got sick because a contrast had been staged. The beautiful woman who prostituted and made veal cutlets in her home with the same dry, yet faithful, regard for ritual was still human to the viewer, maybe finally so, unlike most wives and mothers whose identity Elena vomited up at her own peril.

At pickup, Jake is soaping up his hands. "You're the most beautifulest mom ever. You know what, Toby doesn't have a mom. He's mean to me," he says, looking in the sink, proud of the dirt. I am sitting next to him, corralling his little sister, and quickly make a note in my book to explain ambiguous loss to him later. *Just be nice to kids who don't have what you do and encourage the other kids to share*, is all I can muster. Playing ball with the kids in the park after we all use the toilet I feel like a stranger, a sucker, and too wrapped up in the question as usual. Who has a mother? Strapped and unstrapped for the sixth time today, the car seat is the one to blame and comes between us, it's not me, I swear. I chose to live downtown for a reason, to avoid the desolate anything that creeps up with driving, yet here we are, classic lazy Americans in our station wagon.

On the car radio we hear that girls get more education but not enough leadership roles. Two men are saying Pepsi was a Russian thing, which I remember being my fave in 1989, before we left. We have a mini dance party as we park. Jake likes Weezer, but I don't want him to grow up to be like that guy. I care about art being pure only in the sense that the person making it is less abusive of power than that person is in their public offering.

At home Franny cries. She wants a cape like Jake's. Blankets are not enough. She's naked, running away from me as I change her standing up now, won't fold away luggage at the top body part, and Jake wants to be a naked boy, too, and to play dog. She cries when he knocks her down with the blanket around his shoulders. She tries to grab his penis and then looks down and around her tummy at her vagina. He insists, "Don't touch me unless I have clothes on."

I change Franny sitting down on the kitchen floor and Jake says our kitchen is too small. The radio announces that the Anita Hill trial twenty-year anniversary is upon us and I'm post post being believed myself, as I have said before, liar liar, my pants are stoking a fourth-wave feminism fire.

Mike is not coming home from school until later and I feed the kids the old soup. Save the chops for another day, since they will just suck on the bone and mush the rest to meat juice. Their teeth are like magnets, which are sacred and holy and keep us going round. My stepmother has used magnets on her ailing joints and brittle bones.

I have bought myself five minutes to read the story about Audrie Pott:

On April 11th, seven months after Audrie's suicide, the Santa Clara County sheriff arrested the three boys on charges of misdemeanor sexual battery, felony possession of child pornography, and felony sexual penetration. When they arrested the boys, police seized new phones and other electronic gadgetry their parents had bought to replace what authorities took in the fall. Police found new pictures of other nude teen girls on some of their phones, prompting them to add on new charges in July. Sources close to the case tell *Rolling Stone* that police discovered one of the boys was trying to make money selling the pictures.

If every time a photograph is taken a part of a person's soul gets stolen away we can assume that women are packaged dolls and the only thing they lose is their plastic box so that we can play with them any way we choose.

My daughter wants to wash her doll clothes like a mama does and helps me deposit quarters into the machines at the Laundromat. I offer her my foot to stand on so she doesn't have to be on tippy toes and stretch too hard. "I like to stretch so much," she tells me, one eye scrunched and tongue sticking out.

Franny loves her plastic babies. I consider getting her furniture and grooming supplies for her babies, but I struggle with this. I take a picture of her with one hand on a ministroller with a baby doll that has fallen over to one side. Her other hand is propped up on her chin, looking away from me. Franny's plastic child will outlive her, which is a strange comfort.

Children are obsessed with the tug of possessing and sharing. Hoarding is safety.

My mother, too poor to drink properly, had to steal to survive. Her withdrawals could have killed her. The way my withdrawals from her over the years almost did me in. Too poor in other ways to ask for her, I just pretended she was dead.

In the mornings, I'm trying to deal with my despondency head-on, but every bit of news reminds me of my mother being lost, being raped, being hit, unburied. I am up with the kids and take them to school by myself. By the elevator, my daughter screams in my arms and tries to slide down my torso. She asks for her dad, smelling out my sadness. I distract her from her questions with silly jokes on the way back to our apartment. I interrogate her in a sweet, sarcastic witch voice that is probably way too scary. *Do you love Mama?* She's quiet. She points to her dad.

When I drop Franny off at baby school, she protests and raises her arms up to me. She changes her mind about Daddy and now coils herself around my neck, urging me to stay past the fourth or fifth book I have read her. It never gets easier pulling away so to make myself laugh a little I say, in a thoughtful tone next to her hot cheek, "Franny, you have to stay strong and carry me always in your heart." That's from *The Joy Luck Club*, I think. I didn't come up with that or know why I said it. I don't want to leave her and the more I show my worry the worse the goodbyes get.

XXXX

Back home as I walk by the dresser mirror I realize I'm getting older. *I'm really turning into my mother* says a voice I stamped and forgot to mail off. I don't know what that means because she never got older. I heard the phrase on television many times before and at a coffee shop this morning. But I have no idea if I'm ever going to look more and more like my mother every day. In our Portland apartment I have only this one undated picture of her. A passport photo never used to go anywhere I know of. And I'm so much older than she is in it. Maybe she's going to grow up to look like me is what I think.

I star in this short film as the wiser and bitter one. Having a recurring role is a small comfort. I get to be the parent, always in the waiting room about to get the good news that they found you wandering around by the highway, and once you get fluids and a quick body scan I can take you home and put you to bed. I make a list of ingredients for your favorite soup to keep my hands busy. The magazines in the waiting room say 1989 in neon on curled-up black. Then the plane takes off and everyone is smoking Dunhills, the fancy airport cigarettes for terminal escapists.

My hair began falling out after my daughter's first birthday. Luda says girl children steal your beauty. I know what you're thinking. I already said I am getting older fast. But my hair is too thick, and I like pulling out tangled nets stuck to my feet in the shower. I kiss my daughter goodbye in the morning when she leaves with her dad for baby school. She just learned to lean in and make an *mm mwah* sound. As we make eye contact I tie one of my stray hairs around her ankle or wrist. I hide this act from her. Am I wrapping her in my loss or sharing in my abundance with this ritual? I can't tell, but she obviously has no choice.

My stepmother has a sister, Angela, who needed the protective eye more than most. She upset a woman in her communal flat who was jealous of all the money her heroin-dealing pseudohusband was making. Angela was young like soft cheese when this woman cast an evil eye her way. When Angela moved out of her flat, this witch swept the four corners of my aunt's room and pulled out all the hairs she found in the dustpan. She burned the hair in the middle of the room and stole her good fortune, youth, and beauty. Within two years Angela's man was found dead in the cellar of her building; she was burglarized and robbed of her prized fur coat.

According to my stepmom, the intruders *stripped the blue jeans right off her ass.* I picture it like a silent protest when it was probably more like two burst pipes collapsing under a mallet, or like when my son fights me to get undressed for bed and I grab him by the ankles and pull on the ends of his pants. His thrashing around plugs me into an abstract movie reel of her home invasion.

Angela was strung out on heroin, picking lice off her oily head at the hospital, when her mom had to fly in from Ukraine to rescue her from bad luck. My stepmother said, "Let this be a lesson to you."

And so I teach my daughter to be very careful about where we can let down our hair.

× × × ×

As a child, I spent every summer in the Caucus Mountains. People always ask me if Azerbaijan is mostly Muslim. For some reason I don't remember the people clearly or how they dressed, except the gold teeth, hot tea in tulip-shaped crystal, tarragon syrup with fizzy water, dried fruit, my same coloring, my eyes looking back. Maybe because I was a half-Jew, half-Russian and made no friends and just read books, I didn't yet look for any patterns outside my home. Inside, I closely watched my two uncles get waited on by their scowling mother. They were free men. Unwed. Walking around in their underwear during the scorch of the day. They had their own rooms. They groomed themselves openly. I slept on the couch opposite the couch my granny occupied, both draped over with Persian rugs. She usually wore a head scarf tied around a big low bun, and unwrapped it before bedtime.

When she looked down from the balcony in the night with her hair petting her waist I thought she looked like a witch. If I brushed my hair in the living room she looked at me hard and hissed, "You're shedding. Go brush your hair under the sink like a cat." She was worried about my uncles discovering one of my hairs in their food.

Strays are considered unsanitary.

× × × ×

A tall man with shoulder-length, dark-brown, wavy hair with a nest of gray at the crown enters a bright small bedroom facing Everett Street in Portland's NW quadrant. He's chasing a toddler. The mother of the little girl is lying in bed with a hangover. She just peeled off her contact lenses and the blurry figures make her nausea worse. It's 2:00 p.m. on Mother's Day. She will pull it together by five. The husband has split ends. The wife usually cuts his hair.

I've been doing a survey and the outcome seems to be this: fathers could have done better. Mothers are dead to us if they don't.

× × × ×

I don't drop the kids off at school with Mike the next morning. In our hallway, by the elevator, I say, trying one last time, "Franny, can I tell you a secret?" She nods. I whisper that I love her so much, into her ear. She only says, "Bye." She waves me away and I go pick through a drawer of nursing bras to find one that might fit even though I haven't produced milk in a year. Get ready to start my day with our first goodbye.

I braid Franny's hair, but she screams at me to stop. I comb her hair, but she will only let me do one side. I am almost done tying the band around her pigtail, but she doesn't want me to finish. I can't groom her the way I want to. Can't touch her wild locks. She keeps it for herself, just like her mama holds her mama in secret.

After two years of barely touching her hair I finally realize that she has the same texture and color hair as my mother. Not my black too-full oil-spill locks, but the wispy waves of chestnut brown. This new rejection feels familiar. Familial.

XXXXI

Geophagy, or pica, is an affliction that makes you crave dirt when pregnant. It's your body anticipating or dealing with a sickness and coating the stomach lining with clay to minimize the absorption of a foul substance.

Before we moved to Portland from Cannon Beach I spent many crow and raven seafoam days wondering if I should have another child, or if I should write a book. I found out that I got into graduate school the day after we sheepishly celebrated my fourth pregnancy, which would bring us Franny. I set out to take photos of myself with a tripod in the freezing winter rain and hail in our winter garden beds among the slug-smeared brown vegetation.

A crow cannot count past the number four. If five gunmen shot at the bird, she would take note of each one as she flew away, but she would get lost at five.

The tourist town was usually empty during the week in the off-season and we lived on a dead-end street. When a cord of firewood was delivered to our driveway I waited for my husband to leave in search of surf with our friends and once our son was napping I took off my clothes and ran toward the pile as tall as my husband and as wide as our car. I walked back to the camera, rewound the film and set up the timer, and dove onto the chopped-up trees, inner blond, smelling sweet and tender, splinters shining in the gild of the sun.

My breasts were properly drained, both big and flat, like wads of chewed-up gum spat out on the sidewalk, breasts so well used they have become public. They were rubbed to blue from bearing down on those edges and peaks of wood. I heard a faint laughter of teenage girls from above the big hotel next door as I slid off the pile an hour later. I laid down for the camera one last time and went back inside with my robe on to look at photos of earthquake rubble, shelling rubble, ancient ruins' preserved rubble, and urban decay rubble. I would hug those cold bricks if I could.

Most literature on psychology will say that broken people with attachment disorders and distorted self-images seek escape in sexual acting out. It's intimate touch we should aim for. The more we get to know our lived-in and tousle-haired loved one, sweaty and ripe in our arms, the closer we are to meaningful sex, layered contact, losing oneself the right way. But what if the longer you stay merged and naked the less amorous you feel? What if only space gives arousal the room to rise and knead dough through your belly?

My children are supposed to safely travel through stages of their own. Oral. Anal. Phallic. Latent. Then they get to a finish line of no longer being a child and not yet an adult in the Genital stage. These can't be reverse engineered.

There is a kind of sneaky arousal that happens from living inside *Speedboat.* You can move through Renata Adler without worrying about who is assigned seats in the audience and who has the stage. We are rescuing garbage together through our own version of a neurotic, jangled, and sometimes bone-weary cultural criticism that is half-awake but sober, the unrelenting and indefatigable woman who lives in her not-knowing, the hubris of her directionless days, of brief and scattered musings, her disinterest in being successful and inventing lovers in her solitude, a woman writing and not-writing while she moves in and out of attachments—she lusts and leers.

Orgasms happen in four stages. Excitement, plateau, orgasm, and recovery.

Recovery is what releases the most powerful of bonding drugs—the flood of oxytocin and other feel-good neurochemicals—the "post-orgasmic glow" chemicals are the same ones a mother feels when nursing, kissing, or holding her baby close.

Space aches. But spaces can ache and then explode into new realms.

What if familiarity doesn't breed contempt, but a numbness of the body where it once felt like bears bathing you in a warm river? How can that numbness ever be squared against the dark and un-knowable forest of claws within? The way post-traumatic stress has our brain fixate on the event of terror and won't let up, the way the story remains incoherent, unbelievable, redundant, surreal, and constantly re-lived, but unwanted and discarded like a dirty orphan. The threading of the text, the Morse code messages rap-idly firing out of a foxhole with plenty of white space to breathe, the first line or paragraph hanging on to the bottom of the page, fingers clinging to the edge of a windowsill with a dangling body writhing in the air, rescuing, pointing, moving, not comfortable yet in the company of more paragraphs, challenging transitional space—a page-turner.

Deforestation is something I used to want to take photos of a couple years ago. On my drives to Portland from Cannon Beach I tried to motivate myself to pull over and get out of the car, take my clothes off, set up my tripod, and lie down squarely in the ruins of our local commerce. It was a gestating project about having been a stripper a long time ago and my love of weathered and ruined scenes that get re-staged, re-planted, and re-populated. I wish so badly to be the keeper of the lost and forgotten, of public wastelands.

During most of these commutes it snowed or rained too hard or I was late, or my kids were in the car, or I was ashamed to be found out there, accidentally impaled on the sharp edges of hacked-up trunks. Now the urge is gone. I can only appreciate my old appetite as I speed by, cutting through the fickle weather. A postscript to the giving tree.

Fragment 58 is the fourth almost-complete Sappho poem we have. In it, she complains of old age through allusions to Tithonos and the goddess Eos who rises from the edge of the ocean each dawn to make morning dew from her tears. Because she asked for her lover to be immortal but not to remain young, he grew older and older until he could not lift his arms to care for himself but still held hands with "his deathless wife." Some myths say that he begged to be turned into a cicada tree in the end.

The crooked tree holds no mystery. The storms and the soil are a matter of recorded history.

More and more people have become interested in turning their remains into burial pods to be planted under trees. This way we can be a part of a memory forest instead of a graveyard. But what if the tree you are placed under is diseased or blows down in a storm? Who will collect the poisoned, crumbling wood that has absorbed the loved one's DNA?

In the fourth year of this millennium a new Sappho fragment was discovered around the same time as I missed a connecting flight from Moscow to St. Petersburg on my way to not find you. Scraps of papyrus were found decomposing at a site that was once a municipal dump in Egypt.

When Frances turned two and Jake was six I flew them to the East Coast to visit with their grandparents. This was my daughter's first, and so far only, encounter with my family. It wasn't long before we got into our perennial topic: I was lucky to have an unusual kind of father. Most fathers would have abandoned me in the care of a grandparent with an unfit mother like mine. Men don't usually raise children alone. I was lucky, because if I had stayed behind in Russia, my only fate with no parents to care for me and push me on would have been to become a prostitute. I was lucky to not become a piece of trash in Russia, and I should thank my father every day for that reason alone, instead of keeping score from the past, longed for to be forgotten. Luda is still a bed-skirt mother, hiding Elena away like an impulse purchase from the discount mall.

I asked my stepmother why she thinks my dad lost his temper and physically hurt me so much. Without even thinking about it she explained, "Because you constantly wet your pants, lied about being dirty, and wouldn't change and clean up on your own, just sat in filth."

"Did you guys think that maybe I was just traumatized?"

"*Traumatized* over some no-good whore? And you got a small bladder! There's nothing that could be done about either of those things," my stepmom muses as I look over at my daughter, her diapered bottom on the granite counter. She is not yet potty trained and I am careful to not push her. I learned by losing patience with myself rather than with my son during his road to dryness, to comfort, to control, to safety. I think of what it takes to hurt a child who is unable to use the toilet properly, of how Eva Hesse was beaten by the nuns at the orphanage each time she had an accident, regressed from fleeing war-torn Germany for Holland without her parents. They were able to come fetch her and bring her to America, where she remained dysregulated, hypervigilant, her body betraying her for some time. Screaming wet screams of separation.

Luda, the woman who could have won a Michelle Pfeiffer in *Scarface* look-alike contest in her heyday, is a starling. Not just because she is glamorous, loud, cruel, and shiny. Starlings are nest stealers. Their birdcall is more powerful than a mill saw.

XXXXII

My daughter never wants to wear a jacket, even in the dead of winter. She runs hot.

The Leningrad Blockade reached the height of frigid destitution in January 1944, right before the Germans began their retreat, looting the summer palaces and setting up land mines on their way out. Record numbers of civilians were dying, most getting tired from hunger and falling asleep on the ice on their way to wait in line for paltry cuts of bread. Their petrified bodies were searched for ration cards and loaded onto sleds to be moved aside.

Hope was taking care of her little girl alone that winter. She taught her how to lie very still to conserve energy under the blanket they made by stuffing old sheets sewn together with wood shavings. By the end of that winter siege Hope prayed the child would die already and be spared the suffering of hunger. She would have an unused ration card and an extra portion of bread. Amid her delirium she remembered hiding an egg in a blanket made of various odds and ends. Her own mother taught her that eggs could be made to last longer if stored in wood chips. At the moment she most wished for my granny to disappear, she knelt beside her, tore an opening in the seam, and fished out a lovely egg to save her daughter.

Fourteen years later, Galina became a winter mother. Her daughter never seemed to warm up to motherhood herself. Men go to war needing someone to wait for them. Mothers stay home waiting to be left. All the right kind of mothers raise their kids to leave them.

Whenever I slept over at Granny's house, she cooked me a herring dish called *seledka pad shubeh*—"under fur coat"—and shared her big bed with me. I would curl up in front of her, molding my back against her belly, and wriggle my toes around, trying to worm my way into her flesh. She would collect my icy feet into a little sandwich between her thighs, and the feeling of melting into her lulled me to sleep under the soft blue silk, camel hair–stuffed blanket. The same blanket my mother soiled.

My mother is a cut flower, a bloom crinkling brown on one end and a closed stalk with no water to drink. By what means does this orphan-maker survive? Her child was all daffodils between her thighs. Spilling out yellow. Slimy fungus water on stems in the jar kept too long on a shelf. Her daughter transplanted, transported. A twig re-grafted onto another species of tree.

Too much heat makes a plant bolt. Yellow. Scared. Spent. Gone.

Cut flowers need cold to live. Why do flowers have to dry upside down? Why do they curl up and reach for the ceiling, like a kid who waves their arms toward their mother and insists on being carried no matter what she might be weighed down with already?

I need to know if she's peeing in the snow, like salmon going back home based on their ability to smell out their origins. I need to know if she's cold. But if she's out there lying on top of or underneath the snow is the only question worth asking.

× × × ×

The morning after our trip the kids are still jet-lagged and sleep in while I walk around the apartment unable to get warm, face screaming like a new sunburn, lids too full to open or close properly, thumbs hiding inside the other four chewed-on fingers, and recite the familial details that my father has kept from me until I prodded him into naming the phantom limb. The one that still smolders like a juicy olive on a burning bush. Our kitchen talks ended in a bitter quarrel about my mother. They will not take on the burden of locating Elena, or Elena's remains. My request that they hire a private investigator went unheard, so I called the airline and flew us out on New Year's Eve, arriving at PDX a half hour before midnight thanks to the time change.

Maybe I began to feel this phantom limb when Jake was vacuumed out of me at Woodhull Hospital and I was quartered like a chicken with unusual tears at the sides, as well as the vertical one, making four directions for the midwife to sew back, my left leg so numb from the pinched nerve for months that shaving it felt like prepping someone else for surgery. There was a razor and it touched the skin, but I didn't recognize it as a part of me.

I want to squeeze the life out of each and every one of these baby accordions of shaky letters to see which one survives the mauling. This didn't happen. This did happen. This didn't happen. This happened. A daisy chain. Forget-me-not notes.

A broken circle as a new line. Pluck out the lies. Burn the liar. Trap the wanderer.

The next day, the first day of the year, Portland is unusually sunny and warm, so I take the kids to Couch Park, kicking used hypodermic needles aside. The kids play hide-and-seek by the chestnut tree until it's time to go back in for lunch.

Franny's favorite game when she's carried home is to put sunglasses on my face. *I can't see you.* She lifts them up. Again, and again. *Where are you, baby?*

I found you. She laughs. Found you, Mama.

ACKNOWLEDGMENTS

My book is in your hands because my feminist sister in the struggle, Leni Zumas, tirelessly nurtured and supported its existence until the visionary and truly gutsy Jamie Carr at WME took me under her wing and found us a dream editor, Zack Knoll—to whom I owe mountains of gratitude for providing the mirroring, the questions, the space to grow, and the fanfare to push on through. My dearest family, the ring of cool around my fire pit of writing: Mike Pfaff, who is a real mensch: generous, patient, and kind, as he shares in bringing up Jake and Frances, who have allowed their irreverent and rascally mother to exist as a person. I see you, babies. My passionate, bighearted parents, Gabriel and Luda, who raised me to be the kind of girl who will climb every tree and taste the sweet fruit others left on the highest branch. *Spasibo* to David, Michelle, Chanukah, Anna, and Angela. Dave and Cheryl Pfaff for countless hours of babysitting, stability, and lively shared meals. All of my aunts, uncles, cousins, and distant relatives from the Shalmiyev clan spanning the globe from Germany to Israel, as well as the Pfaffs and

Wilsons for contributing to the robust history of my children's family tree. All of my children's providers of super-competent care and services made it so that I could work on this project, so thank you, kindly.

Mega gratitude to Chris Kraus, who is the reason I dared to write for public viewing. Big thanks to Michelle Tea, Eileen Myles, and Melissa Febos for reading this beast early on and giving it your genius stamp of approval. Michele Glazer, for inspiration, laughter, and new angles for the manuscript. My whole gorgeous PSU MFA community, too large to list here, was and is, invaluable. Everyone at WME, including Matilda Forbes Watson and Caitlin Mahony—a brain hive I am blessed to work with. The Simon & Schuster dream team: Jonathan Karp, Richard Rhorer, Cary Goldstein, Marysue Rucci, Elizabeth Breeden, Alison Forner, Na Kim, Carly Loman, Kayley Hoffman, Shelly Perron, Felice Javit, and Kirstin Berndt. Each and every one of you took my book seriously and worked your magic so the cream could rise to the top when I functioned with zero clues as to how to drive my bus through your many fab lanes.

I am forever grateful to all the old friends, new friends, and my venerable support system. Sarah Roff for taking many leaps of faith, accepting both sides of the coin, and speaking our language. Kelly O'Keefe for knowing our worth and challenging the old to reign in the new. Matt Brose for being my perennial prom date even when he knows where the boys are. Sara Nelson for trusting me and being my oldest friend who writes. Alex Maslansky, who is my brother and book champion. To Jeremy Addam Wilcox for always being so supportive of this project. Ladies of *Visitant*, where bits and pieces of *MW* have appeared. Mary Brearden and Andrea Janda.

ACKNOWLEDGMENTS

Sarah Menkedick at *Vela*. Amy Zimmerman and Todd Gleason of *Drunk In A Midnight Choir,* and *The Literary Review*. My kisses also go to Cooper Lee Bombardier, Jerry Lee, Kari Boden, Will Gruen, Isaac Overcast, Ellie Piper, Megan Fresh, Cassia Gammill, Michelle Kline, Jeanne Tunberg, Sascha Fix, Jennifer Linnman, Megan Labrise, Craig James Florence, and Linda Majors. Thank you to Powell's, Mother Foucault's, Daedalus, and many other independent bookshops that make second homes for us writers. Thank you to anyone who has ever listened to me kvetch, or has allowed me to help you, make you laugh, and cook for you. My biggest wish would be to thank my mother in person and talk to her about my grannies, Chaya and Galina, who are the true heroines of my life.

SELECT BIBLIOGRAPHY

The italicized, slanted, dragging, pushing through a wall, walking toward and away from it all—mothers—was meant to announce, on the dedication page of my book, our many takes on this word: non-uterine, nonlinear, negotiable, collectivized. The notes below are brief and encompass only a fraction of the mothering knowledge gleaned from those who wrote so I could nurse the preceding pages into being. I cannot possibly include and properly thank everyone nesting in my head, but they all continue to rear this obvious child, chapter by chapter. Some of these citations are directly sourced and some are the chorus, the score, the soundtrack, and are woven in throughout the book. Borrowing is a courage. Italics are the flesh in the hands of a midwife. Quotation marks, the placenta.

I

Lorde, Audre. *The Collected Poems of Audre Lorde.* New York: W. W. Norton & Company, 2000. Quoted from "Call," page 417: "Mother, loosen my tongue or adorn me with a lighter burden."

Shire, Warsan. *Teaching My Mother How to Give Birth.* Mouthmark (Book 10). London: flipped eye publishing limited, 2011.

II

Duras, Marguerite. *Duras by Duras.* San Francisco: City Lights Publishers, 1987.

Duras, Marguerite. *The Lover.* New York: Pantheon, 1998.

III

Gessen, Masha. *The Future Is History: How Totalitarianism Reclaimed Russia.* New York: Riverhead Books, 2017.

Mellow, James R. *Charmed Circle: Gertrude Stein and Company.* New York: Henry Holt & Co., 2003.

Shuster, Simon. "Q&A: Masha Gessen Sees a Bleak Future for Putin's Russia." *Time,* October 9, 2017.

Stein, Gertrude. *Brewsie and Willie.* New York: Random House, 1946.

Taubman, William. *Gorbachev: His Life and Times.* New York: W. W. Norton & Co., 2017.

IV

Lorde, Audre. *The Collected Poems of Audre Lorde.* New York: W. W. Norton & Company, 2000. Quoted from "Call," page 417: "Mother, loosen my tongue or adorn me with a lighter burden."

V

Davis, Lydia. *The Collected Stories of Lydia Davis.* New York: Picador, 2010. Page 24 is quoted from the short story "The Thirteenth Woman."

Svenonius, Ian. *The Psychic Soviet.* Chicago: Drag City, 2006.

Svenonius, Ian. *Supernatural Strategies for Making a Rock 'n' Roll Group.* Brooklyn: Akashic Books, 2013.

VI

Aviv, Rachel. "The Trauma of Facing Deportation." *The New Yorker,* April 3, 2017.

VII

Edwards, Elwyn Hartley. *The Horse Encyclopedia.* New York: DK Publishing, 2016.

IX

Millet, Catherine. *The Sexual Life of Catherine M.* New York: Grove Press, 2003.

Nin, Anaïs. *Henry and June: From "A Journal of Love": The Unexpurgated Diary (1931–1932) of Anaïs Nin.* San Diego: Harvest Books, 1990.

Réage, Pauline. *Story of O: A Novel.* New York: Ballantine Books, 2013.

XI

Reid, Anna. *Leningrad: The Epic Siege of World War II, 1941–1944.* New York: Walker & Company, 2011.

XVI

Danchev, Alex. *The Letters of Paul Cézanne.* New York: J. Paul Getty Museum, 2013.
Rilke, Rainer Maria. *Letters on Cézanne.* New York: North Point Press, 2002.

XVII

Fletcher, Alan. *The Art of Looking Sideways.* New York: Phaidon Press, 2001.
Haslett, Tobi. "The Other Susan Sontag." *The New Yorker,* December 11, 2017.
Sontag, Susan. *Debriefing: Collected Stories.* New York: Farrar, Straus and Giroux, 2017.
Unique Japan. "Ma." Explains the various ways "ma" is used in art, music, architecture, and culture. http://new.uniquejapan.com/ikebana/ma/.

XVIII

Sontag, Susan. *Regarding the Pain of Others.* New York: Picador, 2004.

XIX

Adler, Renata. *Speedboat.* New York: NYRB Classics, 2013.
Joyce, James. *Ulysses.* Knoxville, TN: Wordsworth Classics, 2010.
Lorde, Audre. *Zami: A New Spelling of My Name—A Biomythography.* New York: Crossing Press, 1982.
McCarthy, Julie. "How a Lack of Toilets Puts India's Women at Risk of Assault." *Morning Edition*, NPR, June 9, 2014.
Mueller, Cookie. *Walking Through Clear Water in a Pool Painted Black.* Los Angeles: Semiotext(e)/Native Agents, 1990.
Richardson, Dorothy. *Pilgrimage Trilogy: Pointed Roofs, Backwater, Honeycomb.* CreateSpace Independent Publishing Platform, 2018.
Troup Buchanan, Rose. "India Mango Tree Rape Case: Cousins found hanging 'committed suicide' and were not 'sexually assaulted' claim Indian authorities." *Independent* (London), November 27, 2014.

XX

Holy Bible. Peabody, MA: Hendrickson Publishers, 2006.
Barthes, Roland. *A Lover's Discourse: Fragments.* New York: Hill and Wang, 2010.

O'Connor, Sinéad. *I Do Not Want What I Haven't Got.* Ensign/Chrysalis Records, March 20, 1990.

XXI

Barthes, Roland. *Camera Lucida: Reflections on Photography.* New York: Hill and Wang, 2010.
Barthes, Roland. *Mourning Diary.* New York: Hill and Wang, 2012.
Mayer, Bernadette. *The Desire of Mothers to Please Others in Letters.* Brooklyn: Nightboat, 2017.

The common mnemonic "An orphan is left behind, whereas a widow must go alone" is used in typesetting and can be found in *The Chicago Manual of Style.* Used as a metaphor in this chapter.

XXII

Carson, Anne. *Eros the Bittersweet.* Champaign, IL: Dalkey Archive Press, 1998.
Carson, Anne. *If Not, Winter: Fragments of Sappho.* New York: Vintage, 2003. The two books by Carson cited in this chapter are the foundation on which *Mother Winter* was ultimately built and appear throughout.
Dubost, Patrick. "What I Know." Translated by Fiona Sampson. *Poetry,* April 2009.
Farmer, Frances. *Will There Really Be a Morning?* New York: Dell, 1973.
Kraus, Chris. *I Love Dick.* Los Angeles: Semiotext(e)/Native Agents, 1997.
The Jimi Hendrix Experience. *Are You Experienced.* Reprise Records, August 23, 1967.
Mendelsohn, Daniel. "Girl, Interrupted: Who Was Sappho?" *The New Yorker,* March 16, 2015.

XXIII

Carson, Anne. *Eros the Bittersweet.* Champaign, IL: Dalkey Archive Press, 1998.
Carson, Anne. *If Not, Winter: Fragments of Sappho.* New York: Vintage, 2003.
Mendelsohn, Daniel. "Girl, Interrupted: Who Was Sappho?" *The New Yorker,* March 16, 2015.
Thaller, Michelle. *How the Universe Works.* The Science Channel, 2012.

XXVI

Coleridge, Samuel Taylor. "What Is an Epigram?"
Proust, Marcel. *Swann's Way: In Search of Lost Time.* Translation by Lydia Davis. New York: Penguin Classics, 2004.

SELECT BIBLIOGRAPHY

XXVII

Jacobs, Jane. *The Death and Life of Great American Cities*. New York: Vintage, 1992. Also see documentary film: Tyrnauer, Matt, dir. *Citizen Jane: Battle for the City*. 2017; New York, NY: Altimeter Films.

Sullivan, Rosemary. *Stalin's Daughter: The Extraordinary and Tumultuous Life of Svetlana Alliluyeva*. New York: Harper Perennial, 2016.

Yourcenar, Marguerite. *That Mighty Sculptor, Time*. Translation by Walter Kaiser. New York: Farrar, Straus and Giroux, 1993.

XXIX

Kandinsky, Wassily. *Concerning the Spiritual in Art*. San Francisco: Empire Art Press, 2017.

Mayer, Bernadette. *The Desire of Mothers to Please Others in Letters*. Brooklyn: Nightboat, 2017.

XXX

Boss, Pauline. "The Myth of Closure." *On Being*, June 23, 2016.

Brumfiel, Geoff. "Final Report on MH370 Says Failure to Locate Airliner is 'Almost Inconceivable.'" NPR, October 3, 2017.

McCarthy, Julie. "Double Rape, Lynching in India Exposes Caste Fault Lines." *All Things Considered*, NPR, June 2, 2014.

Silverstein, Shel. *The Giving Tree*. New York: Harper & Row, 1964.

Staff Reporting. "When Loved Ones Go Missing, Ambiguity Can Hold Grief Captive." *All Thing Considered*, NPR, March 15, 2014.

XXXI

Babes in Toyland. *Fontanelle*. Reprise Records, August 11, 1992.

Babes in Toyland. *To Mother*. Twin/Tone Records, July 1, 1991.

Danchev, Alex. *Cézanne: A Life*. New York: Pantheon, 2012.

Rewald, John. *Cézanne: A Biography*. New York: Harry N. Abrams, 1986.

An excerpt of the lyrics to "Handsome and Gretel" are:

> My name is Gretel yeah
> I've got a crotch that talks
> And talks to all their cocks
> It's been twelve city blocks you fucking bitch
> Gretel said, oh you feel so bad
> I know you feel so bad

I thought she meant it
Handsome Gretel

I vacuumed out my head
Jumping from bed to bed
My name is Gretel
A soul of metal
My name is Gretel yeah
I've got a sloppy slot

Babes in Toyland had a huge impact on *Mother Winter*. As suggested to me by Leni Zumas, the original title of this book was *To Mother*. It was the sonic and philosophical blend of Carson, Sappho, and Kat Bjelland: a verb and a nod to the epistolary heritage of our foremothers. Please see the Babes' complete discography, as all of their songs hover above and infuse the chapters.

XXXIII

Bair, Deirdre. *Anaïs Nin: A Biography*. London: Trafalgar Square, 1996.
Homer. *The Iliad*. Translation by George Chapman. Knoxville, TN: Wordsworth Classics, 2003.
Lessing, Doris. *The Golden Notebook: A Novel*. New York: Harper Perennial Modern Classics, 2008.
Nin, Anaïs. *Mirages: The Unexpurgated Diary of Anaïs Nin, 1939–1947*. Athens, OH: Swallow Press, 2015.

XXXIV

Barthes, Roland. *A Lover's Discourse: Fragments*. New York: Hill and Wang, 2010.

XXXV

Arcade, Penny. *Bad Reputation: Performances, Essays, Interviews*. Los Angeles: Semiotext(e)/Native Agents, 2009.
Finley, Karen. *Shock Treatment*. San Francisco: City Lights Publishers, 2001.
Fisher, Amy and Robbie Woliver. *If I Knew Then . . .* iUniverse Publishing, 2004.
Higgs, Christopher. "Heroine Worship: Talking with Kate Zambreno." *The Paris Review*, October 22, 2012.
Shocking Blue. "Send Me a Postcard" single. Pink Elephant, 1969.
Van der Kolk, Bessel. *The Body Keeps the Score: Brain, Mind, and Body in the Healing of Trauma*. New York: Penguin Books, 2015.

Wuornos, Aileen. Lisa Kester and Daphne Gottlieb, eds. *Dear Dawn: Aileen Wuornos in Her Own Words*. Berkeley, CA: Soft Skull Press, 2012.

Yousafzai, Malala. *I Am Malala: The Girl Who Stood Up for Education and Was Shot by the Taliban*. New York: Little, Brown and Company, 2013. See XXXI for Babes in Toyland lyric.

XXXVI

Barron, James. "Nation Reels After Gunman Massacres 20 Children at School in Connecticut." *The New York Times*, December 14, 2012.

Dickinson, Emily. *The Gorgeous Nothings: Emily Dickinson's Envelope Poems*. New York: New Directions/Christine Burgin, 2013.

Hunt, Elle. "Chris Kraus: *I Love Dick* Was Written 'In a Delirium.'" *The Guardian*, May 29, 2017.

Kraus, Chris. *Video Green: Los Angeles and the Triumph of Nothingness*. Los Angeles: Semiotext(e)/Active Agents, 2004. Kraus briefly discussed craft and the fiction, autofiction, and memoir conundrum that mostly plagues women who write at a reading in NYC in support of *Video Green* that I attended in 2004.

Lorde, Audre. *Zami: A New Spelling of My Name—A Biomythography*. Toronto: Crossing Press, 1982.

McGaugh, Luther S. *Temple Houston and the Soiled Dove Speech*. CreateSpace Independent Publishing Platform, 2016.

Ono, Yoko. *Grapefruit*. New York: Simon & Schuster, 2000.

Princenthal, Nancy. *Agnes Martin: Her Life and Art*. London: Thames & Hudson, 2015.

Ruefle, Mary. *Madness, Rack, and Honey: Collected Lectures*. Seattle: Wave Books, 2012.

On May 22, 2015, Mary Ruefle was a guest of Portland State University's seminar partnership with Tin House at The Little Church in Portland, Oregon. That Q&A and her reading are cited in this book, covering issues of erasure poems, art, and her famous quote about a poem knocking on her head like the urge to go pee.

Solanas, Valerie. *SCUM Manifesto*. Chico, CA: AK Press, 2013.

XXXVII

Caspar, Barbara, dir. *Who's Afraid of Kathy Acker?* 2008; Austria/Germany: Cameo Film—und Fernsehproduktion.

Engel, Marian. *Bear*. Boston: Nonpareil Books. David R Godine, 2003.

Heraclitus. *The Fragments of Heraclitus*. Overland Park, KS: Digireads Publishing, 2013.

Mitchell, Alanna. *The Spinning Magnet: The Electromagnetic Force That Created the Modern World—and Could Destroy It*. New York: Dutton, 2018.

XXXVIII

Drew, Liam. *I, Mammal: The Story of What Makes Us Mammals.* New York: Blooms-bury Sigma, 2018.

McGaugh, Luther S. *Temple Houston and the Soiled Dove Speech.* CreateSpace Independent Publishing Platform, 2016.

Myles, Eileen. *Afterglow (a dog memoir).* New York: Grove Press, 2017.

I read *Afterglow* in the final stages of editing, instantly struck with the passages about a rapist's mental, spiritual, and psychological demise for breaking open someone's sacred "envelope." The conversations I have with my children about their bodies in this chapter and my own repetitive envelope imagery cross-stitched as a postscript with Myles's book in a way that was eerie and necessary and worthy of citation. You can and do heal, your position may even be that of a forgiver, if you so wish, while an abuser/predator/rapist, an envelope ripper, remains the thief of your mourned safety and innocence, which is a certain kind of death.

Wise Brown, Margaret. *The Runaway Bunny.* New York: Harper & Row, 1942.

XXXIX

Ackerman, Chantal, dir. *Jeanne Dielman, 23 Commerce Quay, 1080 Brussels.* 1975; Belgium/France: Paradise Films.

Burleigh, Nina. "Sexting, Shame and Suicide: A shocking tale of sexual assault in the Digital Age." *Rolling Stone,* September 17, 2013.

Griffin, Susan. *Bending Home: Selected & New Poems 1967–1998.* Port Townsend, WA: Copper Canyon Press, 1998.

Marnell, Cat. *How to Murder Your Life: A Memoir.* New York: Simon & Schuster, 2017.

Tan, Amy. *The Joy Luck Club.* New York: G.P. Putnam's Sons, 1989.

XXXXI

Adler, Renata. *Speedboat.* New York: NYRB Classics, 2013.

De Palma, Brian, dir. *Scarface.* 1983; Burbank, CA: Universal Pictures.

Hesse, Eva. *Diaries.* New Haven, CT: Yale University Press, 2016.

See XXII for Sappho.

XXXXII

See XI for more on the Siege of Leningrad.

*English is my second language—shame-ridden at the start; now, my proud, fast sister, the mile-marker and skin-maker for a vaporized legacy.

ABOUT THE AUTHOR

SOPHIA SHALMIYEV emigrated from Leningrad to NYC in 1990. She is an MFA graduate of Portland State University with a second master's degree in creative arts therapy from the School of Visual Arts. She lives in Portland with her two children. *Mother Winter* is her first book.